Spirit-Filled Singing

"A must-read for every student of worship. *Spirit-Filled Singing* offers a biblical framework for worship leaders of all types and traditions. What better way to seek the Spirit in worship than by modeling our worship leadership after the fruit of the Spirit. I wish I had read this book twenty years ago."

Nathan Drake, Founder, Reawaken Hymns

"A refreshing vision of worship and ministry that offers a fresh perspective and new energy for musicians and worshipers. Drawing from personal experience, church history, broad musical examples, personal reflection, and well-placed humor, Ryanne Molinari's writing breathes new life into our calling, both musically and spiritually."

Dan Forrest, composer; pianist; educator; Artist in Residence, Mitchell Road Presbyterian Church, Greenville, South Carolina

"As both a college chaplain shepherding student worship leaders and a local church musician steeped in weekly congregational life, I find *Spirit-Filled Singing* to be a rare gift—deeply theological, pastorally wise, and musically grounded. Ryanne Molinari beautifully tunes our hearts to the harmony between worship and discipleship, showing how Spirit-filled singing is not just emotional expression but a formation into the fruit-bearing life of Christ. Whether you're leading a worship team, writing songs for your church, or simply longing for more rootedness in your music ministry, this book sings with grace, clarity, and conviction. It's a must-read for those who believe our songs can shape souls."

Bruce Benedict, Worship Arts Chaplain, Hope College; Founder, Cardiphonia Music

Spirit-Filled Singing

Bearing Fruit as We Worship Together

Ryanne J. Molinari

Foreword by Tim Challies

WHEATON, ILLINOIS

Spirit-Filled Singing: Bearing Fruit as We Worship Together

Published by Crossway
1300 Crescent Street
Wheaton, Illinois 60187

Cover design: David Fassett

Cover images: Getty Images; Rawpixel

First printing 2025

Printed in the United States of America

All emphases in Scripture quotations have been added by the author.

Trade paperback ISBN: 978-1-4335-9821-0
ePub ISBN: 978-1-4335-9823-4
PDF ISBN: 978-1-4335-9822-7

Library of Congress Cataloging-in-Publication Data

Names: Molinari, Ryanne J., 1996– author
Title: Spirit-filled singing : bearing fruit as we worship together / Ryanne J. Molinari.
Description: Wheaton, Illinois : Crossway, [2025] | Includes bibliographical references and index.
Identifiers: LCCN 2025003265 (print) | LCCN 2025003266 (ebook) | ISBN 9781433598210 trade paperback | ISBN 9781433598227 pdf | ISBN 9781433598234 epub
Subjects: LCSH: Church music | Music in churches | Public worship
Classification: LCC BV290 .M655 2025 (print) | LCC BV290 `(ebook) | DDC 264/.2—dc23/eng/20250421
LC record available at https://lccn.loc.gov/2025003265
LC ebook record available at https://lccn.loc.gov/2025003266

Crossway is a publishing ministry of Good News Publishers.

VP 34 33 32 31 30 29 28 27 26 25
15 14 13 12 11 10 9 8 7 6 5 4 3 2 1

For the mentors whose maturity and musicianship
showed me eternal beauty.

Contents

Foreword

I SPENT MUCH OF THE PAST TWO YEARS traveling around the world. My journeys took me to many countries across every inhabited continent. And in almost every nation I visited—more than twenty-five of them!—I worshiped with a local church. It was always a church that preached the gospel and honored Scripture while also being deeply embedded in its own culture. Thus, I had the privilege of experiencing a host of musical styles in a host of geographic settings as varied as Northern Europe and Southern Africa, Western Asia and Eastern Australia.

As I reflect on all that I witnessed, heard, and experienced, I find myself more thankful than ever for God's good gift of music and that he both invites and commands us to sing his praises. What a privilege it is to sing psalms and hymns and spiritual songs, with thankfulness in our hearts to God (Col. 3:16)! This is not a privilege God owes us but one he kindly and lovingly grants us.

I have been an avid reader of Christian books for the past twenty-five years, and in that time have read many books on worship. Many authors have scoured Scripture to explain why God tells us to sing and to tell how we can best honor him through our singing. Yet this is not to suggest that everything has been said or that there is nothing left for us to learn! Ryanne Molinari proves this in *Spirit-Filled Singing* by offering something fresh to the discussion and new to our experience of singing to the Lord.

Drawing deeply upon Galatians 5 and Ephesians 5, she makes the fascinating observation that singing and the fruit of the Spirit share a common purpose. Both are to lead to fruitfulness, which is to say, to a life of worship—one that displays our commitment to the Lord and our joy in his salvation. This means that music is not an end in itself but rather a means of bearing fruit.

Many Christians have observed that local churches tend to be more commonly divided by music than by doctrine and that more rifts open up around the songs that are sung than the sermons that are preached. This is grievous to God and ought to be grievous to us, for God's purpose in calling us to sing is to unite us in his Spirit rather than divide us by preference. It is to give us opportunity to bear the fruit of the Spirit rather than the fruit of darkness. It is to prove through the musical harmony of our voices the relational harmony we enjoy as Christians.

I invite every Christian to read this book and, as you read it, to deepen not only your understanding of congregational worship but also your experience of it. May God use this book to help us all bear fruit through the songs we sing!

Tim Challies

Prelude

I DID NOT PLAN to become a church musician. For much of my life, I treated musical worship as tangential—a side gig to supplement my "real" work as a student and professional pianist. I know now that although my technique was forged in the practice room, my heart was formed in choir lofts and sanctuaries, band rehearsals and early services.

I learned the way of love in a church choir and joy through the cheerful suffering of a dear mentor. I enjoyed peace in the silence between songs and learned patience through the slow, steady rhythms of old hymns. I experienced kindness in the encouragement and honesty of devoted teachers. I discovered theological and aesthetic goodness in an array of musical genres. I cultivated faithfulness by practicing when my hands were cold and the church was empty. I am developing gentleness (not my most natural virtue) by laboring as a servant more than a leader and am exercising self-control by surrendering to the conductor of my life, the composer of my song.

Now I am a professional musician, working with secular and sacred ensembles, but my career has become secondary to my worship. I spent years thinking that working in worship was preparing me to be a better musician. Now I know that working in music was preparing me to be a better worshiper. Years of studying, practicing, and serving have rendered me a ready instrument in God's hands, equipping me to play music but, more importantly, to bear fruit.

Introduction

Bearing Fruit and Singing Songs

Do not get drunk with wine, for that is debauchery, but be filled with the Spirit, addressing one another in psalms and hymns and spiritual songs, singing and making melody to the Lord with your heart.

EPHESIANS 5:18–19

MY FAVORITE PART of a symphony takes place before the actual performance. I love listening as the musicians warm up—as multiple sounds and rhythms intermingle at random. Then the magic begins: The concertmaster stands, and everyone tunes to a unified pitch. Whatever follows, this moment is crucial; it establishes the common tone that is essential for harmonious artistry.

I fear that we tend to go about musical worship like an orchestra that has forgotten to tune. Beautiful sounds emerge, excellent musicians shine, and catchy lyrics are proclaimed—but where is the common tone? Where is the shared vision that can be traced back to the first Christians and persists today in many distinct genres and forms?

Musical worship—intended to reflect and reinforce the "perfect harmony" of believers—has become one of the most dissonant parts of church life. One pastor I know commented, "Rarely do I have someone approach me after a sermon to criticize a fine point of my theology, but someone will usually complain about the music." Too often, musical worship is undermined by dissension, rivalry, and pride—the "works of the flesh" rather than the "fruit of the Spirit" (Gal. 5:19–25). Like a fractured ensemble, the church's musical worship needs a tuning. Worship leaders, teams, and congregations need a shared vision that will withstand the test of time and accommodate evolving musical styles as well as the diverse gifts, resources, and contexts of individual churches. Put simply, we need an approach to musical worship that is scripturally faithful and situationally flexible—neither chaotic nor constricting. In doctrinal terms, we need a vision not characterized by legalism or license.

This leads us to *fruitfulness.*

Ephesians 5: Spirit-Filled Singing

I write all over my music, planning every phrase. Once, I saw another musician's sheet music with only "see where the Spirit leads" scrawled across the top. This musician correctly intuited that singing is a ministry of the Holy Spirit.

Because we tend to associate worship with music, it might seem that we make too much of singing. Worship is certainly more than singing, but it is not less. Scripture is clear that singing is not an optional subtype of worship but an initiation into a life of worship. Writing to the Ephesian Christians to encourage their unity and morality, Paul does not just send a list of rules to follow but commands them to sing to and with one another (Eph. 5:18–19). Why? Because worshipful singing and godly living are inextricably linked as ministries of the Spirit.

In Ephesians 5:18–21, one of the most well-known passages on singing, fruitfulness is front and center. Earlier in this chapter, Paul calls Christians to reject "the unfruitful works of darkness" and to pursue "the fruit of light [that] is found in all that is good and right and true" (Eph. 5:9–11). Paul begins Ephesians 5 with a call to love, the first and greatest fruit of the Spirit.

Figure 1 charts the overarching argument of Ephesians 5.

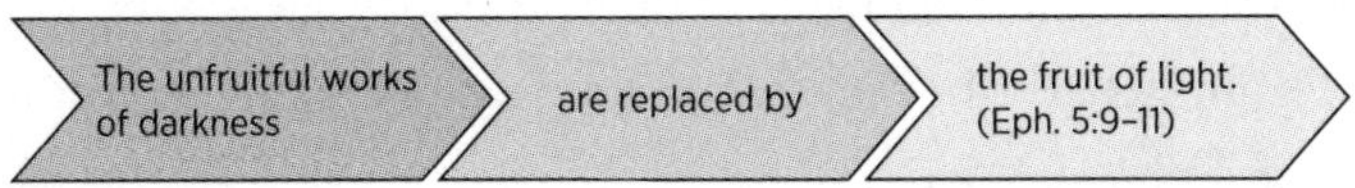

Fig. 1.

But Paul does not simply tell the Ephesians to exchange unfruitfulness for fruitfulness and then abandon them to their own devices. He includes specific instructions:

> Do not get drunk with wine, for that is debauchery, but be filled with the Spirit, addressing one another in psalms and hymns and spiritual songs, singing and making melody to the Lord with your heart, giving thanks always and for everything to God the Father in the name of the Lord Jesus Christ. (Eph. 5:18–20)

To help the Ephesians pursue righteousness, Paul prescribes two things: (1) Be filled with the Spirit and (2) sing to and with one another. Being filled with the Spirit leads to congregational singing, but singing in itself is not the end. Instead, being filled with the Spirit leads to singing and, through singing, fruitfulness.

We find an interesting contrast in this chapter between drunkenness and being "filled with the Spirit" and between debauchery and singing. To be filled with the Spirit is the fruitful alternative to being filled with wine, and singing together is the spiritual alternative to sinning together. Just as debauchery is the result of drunkenness, singing is the result of being filled with the Spirit. This call to song flows from the call to "walk in love" in verse 2 and the call to sobriety in verse 18. In this, singing is directly connected with the first and final fruits of the Spirit: love and self-control.[1]

Figure 2 charts the progression from unfruitfulness to fruitfulness in Ephesians 5:1–21.

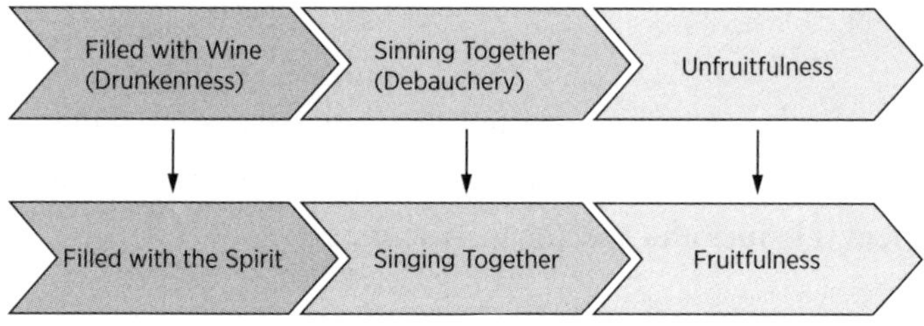

Fig. 2.

As a Scripture-ordained, Spirit-filled activity, singing together represents the heart of worship. It replaces sinful behavior and helps cultivate the fruit of the Spirit. We often take for granted

1 Lane T. Dennis and Wayne Grudem, eds., *ESV Study Bible: English Standard Version* (Crossway, 2016), 2271.

that how we live influences how we sing. Here, Scripture proclaims the surprising truth that how we sing should affect how we live—whether according to the Spirit or according to the flesh.

Galatians 5: The Fruit of the Spirit

You are probably familiar with the "fruit of the Spirit" listed in Galatians: love, joy, peace, patience, kindness, goodness, faithfulness, gentleness, and self-control. Perhaps you memorized these virtues as I did: through song. Indeed, many of us were introduced to theology through children's songs. And why not? What we sing becomes ingrained in our minds and hearts, infiltrating our affections, behavior, and character. As Ephesians 5 reveals, the Holy Spirit works through our singing for the sake of fruitfulness.

Together, Galatians 5:1–26 and Ephesians 5:1–21 present singing and fruitfulness as joint products of the Holy Spirit. Like Ephesians 5, Galatians 5 hinges on a call to love (Gal. 5:13–14). Then, as with the Ephesians, Paul convicts the Galatians of the "works of the flesh" (5:19) and offers the alternative: the fruit of the Spirit (5:22–23).

In Ephesians, being filled with the Spirit leads to singing, which contributes to upright, harmonious living. In Galatians, living "in step with the Spirit" produces the fruit of the Spirit (Gal. 5:25). Singing and fruitfulness function similarly. Both testify to and reinforce the ministry of the Spirit in our lives, with singing together as a means of fostering fruitfulness.

Colossians 3: Sing Songs, Bear Fruit

Singing and the fruit of the Spirit are evident together in Colossians. Like Ephesians and Galatians, Colossians includes a list of sinful works to "put to death" (Col. 3:5) and identifies what Christians should do and how they should be characterized instead. Rather than concluding that we must sing or bear fruit, however, Colossians 3:12–17 synthesizes these ministries of the Spirit as it encourages Christians to bear fruit *in and through* singing.

Colossians 3:16 reads, "Let the word of Christ dwell in you richly, teaching and admonishing one another in all wisdom, singing psalms and hymns and spiritual songs, with thankfulness in your hearts to God." Ephesians portrays singing as a way of reinforcing righteous living, and Colossians indicates that this is because singing is an essential teaching tool, a way of working God's word into our hearts.

The fruit of the Spirit also abounds in Colossians 3. Kindness and patience are listed directly, as is the peace of Christ (3:12–13, 15). Love is identified as the fruit that "binds everything together" (3:14). Gentleness appears as "meekness," its most common synonym (3:12). Joy is found in thankfulness, which generates rejoicing (3:15). Goodness is active in the command to "teach and admonish one another in all wisdom," and to let the word "dwell in you richly" (3:16). Faithfulness pervades the qualifier, "whatever you do, in word or deed" (3:17). Self-control permeates the entire passage, which calls Christians to put their old ways to death and to don a new self (3:12).

The parallels between Ephesians 5, Galatians 5, and Colossians 3 reveal that Spirit-filled people abound with fruitfulness and singing—and, indeed, fruitfulness through singing. Figure 3 summarizes these parallels.

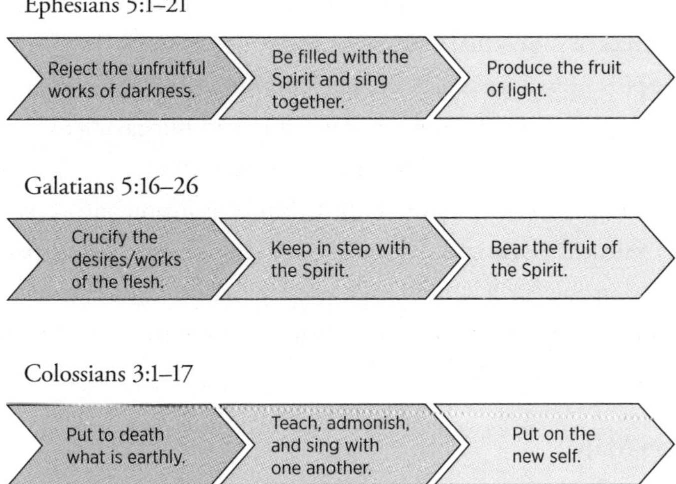

Fig. 3.

Ultimately, the purpose of singing and fruitfulness is the same: worship. Both flow from the ministry of the Holy Spirit and are intended to edify the church and glorify God. In this sense, singing can be considered another fruit (product) of the Spirit. Jesus says, "By this my Father is glorified, that you bear much fruit and so prove to be my disciples" (John 15:8). According to Jesus, bearing fruit glorifies the Father. Our singing is at its best—its most worshipful and God-honoring—when it fosters fruitfulness.

Why, then, do we not think in terms of fruitfulness when we sing? Why not allow the fruit of the Spirit to shape our musical worship?

The fruit of the Spirit provides a more enduring, biblical standard than relevance or even tradition. At the same time, this approach is gracious enough to inform churches of all styles and contexts. It is true to the Spirit it reflects as it encourages unity in the body of Christ without dismissing the unique gifts and resources of individual Christians and congregations. The fruit of the Spirit provides a much-needed "common tone" for evaluating, engaging, and executing musical worship without caving to chaos or imposing extrabiblical restrictions on creativity.

We have too long stewed in unfruitful confusion and division over musical worship. Like the organ at my church, we are painfully overdue for a tuning. We need a harmonious framework for singing as the church—one that is guided by Scripture and surrendered to the Spirit.

Road Map

Good worship leaders provide "road maps" to guide their bands through complex songs. Likewise, I want to provide an overview of the chapters ahead so you can read this book in the way that is most helpful for you. The following nine chapters examine the fruit of the Spirit as listed in Galatians 5:22–23. Each chapter defines a particular fruit and exposits related ideas that may influence our worship as both leaders and laypeople. I also explore how music-making has the unique capacity to communicate and cultivate each fruit in and beyond corporate worship.

If you are a musician or technician, I know you'll be itching to practice what you learn. Each chapter includes real-life examples and concludes with questions for reflection, discussion, and application. As you walk through these questions, remember that Spirit-filled singing is not about conforming to a one-size-fits-all method. Instead, it is about biblically and prayerfully discerning what will be most helpful for your people as they seek to live in the Spirit, look more like Christ, and glorify the Father.

Because musical worship is meant to be a communal activity, I hope you'll consider reading this book with others. I've structured it to serve as a nine-to-eleven-week curriculum suitable for upper high school and undergraduate music students, church study or staff groups, and worship teams (traditional, contemporary, or blended). However you choose to read it, I pray that this resource provides ample food for thought and discussion, drawing you and your fellow worshipers closer together in song and Spirit.

To enhance the musicality of this book, I conclude each chapter with a closing hymn. For copyright purposes, these are public domain hymns. To compensate for the lack of contemporary songs, I've included a QR code in the back matter that links to a Spotify playlist to accompany your reading. This playlist includes a greater variety of genres and is intended as a musical "commentary" on the fruit of the Spirit, offering song recommendations for private devotion and public worship.

For simplicity's sake, I use "musical worship" holistically to refer to elements including (but not limited to) composition, production, leadership, and participation. I will specify when necessary, but my goal is to provide general principles that can be applied to your unique role and context.

Finally, I understand how busy the life of a worship leader or church musician can be—especially as many of us are multivocational—but I hope you will walk through each chapter and question, even if it is slow going. Patience is a fruit of the Spirit, after all.

And now may you be filled with the Holy Spirit, encouraged and equipped to make music and bear fruit.

Reflection/Discussion

1. What is your involvement in musical worship? How has musical worship influenced your spiritual formation?

2. If you had to describe your vision for music ministry in one word, what would it be and why?

3. Which fruit of the Spirit do you most associate with musical worship? The least?

4. Which fruit most characterizes your worship? Which needs the most growth?

5. Which fruit of the Spirit is most characteristic of your worship team or congregation? Which fruit(s) need tending?

1

Love

Establishing the Root

For this reason I bow my knees before the Father . . . that you, being rooted and grounded in love, may have the strength to comprehend with all the saints what is the breadth and length and height and depth, and to know the love of Christ that surpasses knowledge, that you may be filled with all the fullness of God.

EPHESIANS 3:14–19

I WAS ONCE ASKED to test a freshly delivered grand piano. It had been placed in an airy sanctuary, with sunshine filtering in from a perfect summer's day. Aware of only a few people going about their weekday tasks, I launched into one of my favorite pieces: Dan Forrest's magnificent arrangement of "How Great Thou Art." I soared through the piece, conscious that it was the best I had ever played and reveling in the beautiful instrument and setting. As I played, I was vaguely aware of a figure standing in the doorway, listening. Now playing to an audience, I nearly sang along: "Then sings my soul, my Savior, God, to Thee: How great Thou art!"

I let the sound waves echo after the final cadence. Then I tried to sneak away as though I had not just played very loudly in an ordinarily quiet space, but before I could leave, I was approached by the figure from the doorway. I recognized her as the woman who, on my first Sunday at this church, informed me that she hated traditional worship. As a traditional worship leader, you can imagine how well I took that.

This time, she approached with her guard down. Weeping, she hugged me and explained that she hated that hymn most of all. As she shared some of her story, I was horrified to learn that a hymn I associated with joyful praise had been the soundtrack of childhood abuse at the hands of a pastor and father figure. Without meaning to, I nearly forced her to relive this trauma, and it is only by the grace of the Holy Spirit—the Comforter—that my music played a part in mending rather than reopening her wounds.

"I don't like traditional worship, but I like you," she continued straightforwardly. She told me that listening to me play helped her enjoy that old, scarred hymn for the first time. I was struck. Risking her comfort, she had listened to me play one of my favorite pieces. In doing so, she loved me even as I unintentionally failed to love her. Marvelously, as the Spirit comforted her and convicted me, he knit us closer together in the love of Christ.

This moment was pivotal. It forced me to reckon with the reality that what is a hymn to me may be a hurt to another. The apostle

Paul compares loveless talent to tuneless, intemperate, deafening noise. Even our best music, without Christlike love, is nothing more than "a noisy gong or a clanging cymbal" (1 Cor. 13:1).

The Firstborn Fruit

The first fruit of the Spirit is not just love but a specific type of love: *agapē*. When the New Testament was being written, the word *agapē* was distinctly Christian. There is little trace of this word in the Greek polytheistic literature of the time and the more one learns about *agapē*, the more countercultural it seems today as well.[1] In a culture that seeks to define love by itself ("Love is love") or as attraction and affirmation, *agapē* stands unique as a concrete, observable, active type of love—a Christlike love.

Agapē is most generally defined as "the quality of warm regard for and interest in another" with proposed synonyms including "esteem" or "affection."[2] But these English terms do not capture the comprehensive nature of this love. For a fuller picture of *agapē*, we must turn to Scripture.

Agapē appears 116 times in the Greek New Testament, with nine of these occurrences (a relative majority) in 1 Corinthians 13. You are likely familiar with this chapter, but it is worth dwelling in before continuing through this book. Not only does it paint a portrait of *agapē* but it does so by describing the fruit of the Spirit in its entirety. First Corinthians 13 describes love in terms of the following:

1 Frederick William Danker, ed., *A Greek-English Lexicon of the New Testament and Other Early Christian Literature*, 3rd ed. (University of Chicago Press, 2000), 6; hereafter, BDAG.

2 BDAG 6.

- Joy: Love "rejoices with the truth" and "hopes all things" (13:6, 7).
- Peace: Love "does not insist on its own way" and "is not irritable or resentful" (13:5).
- Patience: Love "bears all things" (13:4, 7).
- Kindness: Love is kind and does not boast (13:4).
- Goodness: Love "does not envy" and "does not rejoice in wrongdoing" (13:4, 6).
- Faithfulness: Love "believes all things, hopes all things, and endures all things" (13:7).
- Gentleness: Love "is not arrogant or rude" (13:4–5).
- Self-control: Love pursues clarity and maturity (13:11–12).

This reading of 1 Corinthians 13 suggests that love is not only the first and greatest fruit of the Spirit but is itself *the* fruit of the Spirit. Thus, another way to punctuate Galatians 5:22–23 might be with a colon rather than a comma: "The fruit of the Spirit is love: joy, peace, patience, kindness, goodness, faithfulness, gentleness, and self-control."[3] Love is not just listed first among the fruit; it *is* the fruit. When we talk about *agapē*, we are talking about the fruit of the Spirit, and when we consider the fruit of the Spirit, we are considering the character of *agapē*.

Although each chapter in this book considers an individual "fruit" of the Spirit, the fruit is essentially singular. It's a cohesive unit, contained within and sprouting from love. Just as we cannot define love apart from the fruit, we cannot pursue any fruit apart from love. To sing joyfully is to revel in God's love. To be

3 *NET Bible: Full Notes Edition*, 2nd ed., ed. W. Hall Harris (Thomas Nelson, 2019), at Gal. 5:22.

patient with others' skill levels is to practice love. To sing with self-control—with focus and intentionality—is to prioritize and protect love. As we grow in our understanding and application of the fruit of the Spirit, we grow in love.

True Vine, Good Soil

Paul describes love as "the greatest" of the theological virtues: faith, hope, and love (1 Cor. 13:13). The word for "greatest" (*megas*) means "superior" or "sublime."[4] This specific form (*meizōn*) is comparative, emphasizing that love is not only great but "*the* greatest." In other places, the root of "greatest" carries connotations of eldership, maturity, and the authority of age.[5] Because of this, we can think of love as the "firstborn" fruit of the Spirit; it precedes and produces the others.

Thinking of love as the "firstborn" fruit also points us to its source: Christ, "the firstborn of all creation," who is "before all things and in him all things hold together" (Col. 1:15–17). Love is the root of the fruit, and Christ is the root of love. He is the true vine and, to love well, we must abide in him. When Paul prays for the Ephesians to be "rooted and grounded in love," it isn't just because love is a nice feeling; it's because our entire existence—our lives, worship, and fruitfulness—will wither apart from the love of Christ (Eph. 3:17). John 15:1–17 abounds with fruitfulness language, and Jesus is clear: we cannot bear fruit without being steeped in his love.

I was raised in Arizona and spent many years trying desperately to sustain a garden. Nothing worked, and my plants inevitably died. When I moved to Iowa, I planted seedlings without much

4 BDAG 624.

5 "Μέγας," Bill Mounce website, accessed September 2, 2024, https://www.billmounce.com/greek-dictionary/megas.

hope. To my surprise, vines nearly took over my yard, and my husband had to stop me from opening a pumpkin patch (I have a black cat and play the organ, so it seemed fitting). The difference was not in my level of care or the quality of the plants themselves: it was the soil. Good, rich Midwestern soil.

Our first occupation as worshipers is this: bury ourselves deep in the good soil of Christ's love. Only then can we abound with fruit. Our source of love cannot be how many people praise our singing, download our new single, view our online service, or sign up for choir. We can rely only on the love of God in Christ Jesus, and we will worship most lovingly when we abide deepest in him. The more we lean into the perfect love—the full fruitfulness—of our true vine, the better prepared we will be to bear fruit in and beyond our worship.

Music-Making and Community-Building

We are inundated with love songs. Love (or the feelings people identify as love) is by far the most popular subject of songwriting, so much so that I am thrilled whenever I find a secular artist who sings about more than romance. In reality, though, every song is a love song. The question is, Who or what is the object of that song's love? And what sort of love is it? At its core, musical worship is an expression and enforcement of our love for God. We praise him because we love him, and in praising him, we fan the flames of this love.

Singing together is also an opportunity to love one another. In Ephesians 5 and Colossians 3, Paul exhorts Christians to love one another and concludes by telling them to sing together. This is not coincidence but providence. Even beyond church music, group music-making has always been a distinctive of human community. It is universal to all tongues, tribes, and nations. However materialists try to explain this, Christians understand that God made us relational creatures. He also made us singing creatures and graciously gives us music as a way of relating to one another.

In one study, researchers measured the respiration and heart rate variation of a group of singers. They had the participants hum individually in their own time. Then participants sang the hymn "Fairest Lord Jesus" together. Singing a steady, structured song—as opposed to humming individually—caused participants' respiration and heart rates to become more similar. Isn't this a beautiful image of how the church's worship should be? All the members of Christ's body, breathing with one Spirit and beating with one heart as they join in praise.

The researchers from this study concluded that when individuals sing together, they become more physiologically unified and may thus also be better prepared to uphold shared perspectives.[6] Put simply, singing forces us to breathe together as we participate in a common rhythm and proclaim the same phrases. Naturally, this requires us to adapt to, rely on, and relate to one another. This cooperation tends to then transcend music-making to influence community-building—transposing individual singers into a choir.

Singing together propels us into relationship with one another. It prods us toward love.

The Most Excellent Way

If music-making fosters community, how much more should musical worship promote love in the body of Christ? And yet, let's

6 Björn Vickhoff et al., "Music Structure Determines Heart Rate Variability of Singers," *Frontiers in Psychology* 4 (2013), https://doi.org/10.3389/fpsyg.2013.00334.

be realistic: musical worship tends to cause as much division as it does unity and as much contention as it does charity. This is and should be concerning. Without love, our worship becomes hypocrisy. Remember the "clanging gongs"? Although loud percussion is common in worship and Scripture repeatedly encourages the use of cymbals, the idea of a "clanging gong" implies something arrogant, insensitive, and deafening—something that hinders rather than helps our praise.

By contrast, there is nothing more beautiful than Christians living and worshiping together in love. In his letter to the Ephesians, Ignatius of Antioch writes that in "concord and harmonious love, Jesus Christ is sung."[7] We have two choices in our approach to worship. We will either produce discordant noise or resonate with the love of Christ.

Let's return to 1 Corinthians. In chapter 12, Paul explains that our gifts must be used for the building up of the body. We cannot rely on our musical prowess or leadership capabilities. These things are worth stewarding with diligence and gratitude, but love remains "a still more excellent way" (1 Cor. 12:31). Paul goes so far as to say that without love we not only "gain nothing" but "are nothing" (13:1–3). Again, this is no abstract, worldly love but the fruitful love of God in Christ, imparted to us by the Spirit.

I am perpetually delighted that God chose to make mankind a singing species. Music-making is integral to our nature and relationships. It may even be part of what it means to be made

7 Ignatius, *Epistle to the Ephesians*, in The Ante-Nicene Library, vol. 1: *The Apostolic Fathers*, ed. Alexander Roberts and James Donaldson (T&T Clark, 1870), 149–50. Quoted by Steven R. Guthrie, "The Wisdom of Song," in *Resonant Witness: Conversations Between Music and Theology*, ed. Jeremy S. Begbie and Steven R. Guthrie (Eerdmans, 2011), 384.

in God's image, for God is described as singing lovingly over his people (Zeph. 3:17). The first instance of human community—when God forms Eve from Adam's rib—is celebrated in poetry, perhaps even song (Gen. 2:23). But music-making alone is not enough to knit our churches together; we need love. Lead worship at any church for five minutes, and you'll know that singing by itself is not enough to cultivate genuine *agapē*. Instead, we have to intentionally pursue love in its fullness—that is, joy, peace, patience, kindness, goodness, faithfulness, gentleness, and self-control—as we sing.

At one church I served, the leader regularly programmed a song I found (frankly) annoying. There was nothing unbiblical about it; it just didn't appeal to me. My fleshly instinct was to refuse to sing, and maybe even grimace a bit to show my distaste. There are two problems with this: (1) It's petty and selfish; we don't have to love a song to love its singers. (2) By not singing, I was cutting myself off from the very thing that might increase my love!

Once I realized this, I forced myself to sing along. The moment I opened my mouth, I began to feel less critical. I began to soften—if not toward the song, at least toward those singing it. As I joined in, I prayed for those around me, asking the Lord to use this song to help them abide in his love. And guess what? As I sang out of love for God and others, I began to feel that same love more deeply. I even began to move a little to the song, almost enjoying it. As I devoted my breath to the same choruses as the rest of that dear church, I felt my heart tune to the love of Christ even—and perhaps especially—as I sang my least favorite song.

Jesus laid down his life for us and calls us to love like him, even dying for others (John 15:12–13). If we are unwilling to lay aside our preferences for three minutes once a week to serve others by singing a song we aren't keen on, we are kidding ourselves if we think we would die for them. If you have the option of attending and serving a biblical church that uses your favorite music, you have the freedom to do so. But if you are unwilling to engage another style of worship, I encourage you to examine yourself: Are you singing (or not singing) out of self-love or sacrificial love? Are you loving your favorite genre or are you loving God, who desires the unity of his people?

If you're reading this book, you probably love music. Musical worship, though, is not merely about doing what we love but about loving the Lord and our neighbors—those singing beside us. *Agapē* calls us to look beyond ourselves, to deepen and strengthen our relationships as we sing together.

Remember the Root

What do plants and chords have in common? Roots. Puns aside, both plant and musical roots provide an analogy for how love operates in the Christian life. We've already established that love is the firstborn and "root" of the fruit of the Spirit. We have also considered how group music-making can image and increase our love. Now, music theory has a few remarkable things to teach us about love as our root.[8]

The Root Provides Identity

In music theory, the "root" is the note by which a chord is named (C is the root of a C chord, G the root of a G chord, and so on).

8 Portions of this section first appeared on my website, Ryanne Molinari, "Three Ways Musical Roots Teach Us About Love," *Ryanne Molinari* (blog), July 14, 2023, https://ryannemolinari.com/.

It is the foundational pitch that gives the chord its identity. This sounds familiar. In John 13:34–35, Jesus says, "A new commandment I give to you, that you love one another: just as I have loved you, you also are to love one another. By this all people will know that you are my disciples, if you have love for one another."

Like a chord named for its root, we are to be identifiable as Christians because we live out the love of Christ. This is at once a calling and a comfort. It means that we must examine our lives and worship to see whether they are conveying Christlike love. But it also offers this profound consolation: Our deepest identity has already been bestowed on us. We are beloved by and in Christ. It is out of this most precious identity that we sing.

Even as believers, it is easy to get caught up in titles, obligations, and ambitions. We must combat this by returning to our root—by remembering that our identity in Christ precedes and supersedes our roles as worship directors and musicians. We are beloved members of Christ's body and bride first and worship leaders second. The love of God in Christ is our foremost identity.

The Root Provides Structure and Clarity

There's a reason many songs use a similar chord progression: I (tonic)–V–vi–IV–I (tonic). As a very poor guitarist, I appreciate this norm! If we assume our starting chord is the tonic (the chord built on the root of the scale) and want to end our song solidly in the same key, the middle parts often work themselves out. The root is not just the primary note in a chord; it's the anchor. The root of a tonic chord provides a point of reference for all other chords and notes. If you play the chord progression above without starting or ending on the tonic chord, it will sound odd. A sense of order will be missing, and the three middle chords will feel random. So it is, too, when we try to worship without the love of Christ constantly behind and before us. The trick to hearing different chords as a harmonious progression is to keep the root or tonic in your mind—mentally tuning to it even when it is not being played.

Worship leaders often work more than one job. Even full-time worship leaders have to balance multiple roles and responsibilities: audiovisual coordinator, instrument technician, band leader, choir director, songwriter, arranger—the list goes on and on. As with chord progressions, however, the key to navigating the various aspects of our ministry and worship is the same: Keep the love of Christ always at the forefront of your mind and remember that no aspect of your worship and ministry is beyond the scope of this love. In seasons of seeming chaos, listen intently for the root. The love of Christ prevails and will see you through. He is holding all things together.

The Root Provides the End

To our Western ears, a piece of music is not really finished until it returns to the tonic chord in root position. If you play the chord progression in the previous section, you will hear how the harmonies lean toward the tonic. There is tension until you reach the final chord, which is also the first chord. In the same way, love is the beginning and end of our lives as Christians. Every part of us should yearn toward the love of God like dissonance seeking resolution. Accordingly, godly love—the fruit of the Spirit—must direct every decision we make.

While memorizing a Bach prelude, one of my students got lost in the music. Some students would have started over or given up, but she had a firm grasp of an essential principle of music performance: When in doubt, find the root. After some dissonant meandering, her harmonic decisions began to make sense. Remembering that she was in the key of C, she began to emphasize notes that would guide her to the dominant chord (G) and, finally, the tonic chord with a C octave as its root. It was not the path Bach wrote, but she ended in the right place.

If you feel directionless or overwhelmed in your life, ministry, or worship, go back to the basics. Remember the root. Our loving Savior does not demand genius or virtuosity, although these can certainly be to his glory. Instead, he simply asks us to use our gifts to love him and his people. This is the goal of our worship. When all else grows complicated, love is the end we must pursue (1 Cor. 14:1).

The Root Provides Unity

A musical note is actually a collection of frequencies that our ears interpret as a single pitch. I can think of no better image for the fruit of the Spirit as love than this: striking a key on the piano or plucking a guitar string and knowing that within the vibrations we hear are multiple pitches, all singing yet sounding together as one perfectly tuned note.

The fruit of the Spirit is not fragmented, as if some of us are peace plants or kindness cacti or faithfulness flowers. Instead, the fruit of the Spirit in our worship should sound forth as a harmonious, unified whole—a cornucopia of inseparable fruits or a pristine nine-voice chord. When we sing with joy, peace, patience, kindness, goodness, faithfulness, gentleness, and self-control, it should sound—simply and beautifully—like love.

Closing Hymn: "O the Deep, Deep Love of Jesus"

Reread Ephesians 3:14–19, the passage featured at the beginning of this chapter. If that doesn't make you want to sing, I don't know what will. As we root our singing deep, deep in the love of Christ, I hope you'll join me in this "closing hymn." The tune most commonly used for this hymn ("Ebenezer") is one of my favorites. It features driving triplets and a determined mood that combine perfectly with the text to convey the tenderness and fierceness of God's love. A recording of this hymn is included in the "Spirit-Filled Listening" playlist, which can be accessed using the QR code or URL at the back of the book.

Oh, the deep, deep love of Jesus—
Vast, unmeasured, boundless, free—
Rolling as a mighty ocean
In its fullness over me!
Underneath me, all around me
Is the current of his love—
Leading onward, leading homeward
To his glorious rest above.

Oh, the deep, deep love of Jesus—
Spread his praise from shore to shore!
Praise his mercy, praise his goodness;
Praise his love forevermore.
How he watcheth o'er his loved ones,
Died to call them all his own;
How for them he intercedeth,
Watcheth o'er them from his throne.

Oh, the deep, deep love of Jesus—
Love of ev'ry love the best—
'Tis an ocean vast of blessing;
'Tis a haven sweet of rest.
Oh, the deep, deep love of Jesus—
'Tis a heav'n of heav'ns to me;
And it lifts me up to glory,
For it lifts me up to thee.[9]

Reflection/Discussion

1. Have you ever thought about the fruit of the Spirit as love?

2. How does love produce and reinforce joy, peace, patience, kindness, goodness, faithfulness, gentleness, and self-control?

3. Do you agree that singing can help "knit us together" in love?

4. Read 1 Corinthians 13 but replace "love" with "my singing" or "my worship." Are these verses still true? Based on this exercise, how might you be failing to convey love in your worship?

5. If you are a worship leader, repeat the above exercise. This time, substitute "my team" or "my church's worship" for "love." In what ways might your team or congregation need to be rooted deeper in love?

9 S. Trevor Francis, "O the Deep, Deep Love of Jesus!," Hymnary.org, 1890, https://hymnary.org/.

2

Joy

Singing *con Grazia*

If you keep my commandments, you will abide in my love, just as I have kept my Father's commandments and abide in his love. These things I have spoken to you, that my joy may be in you, and that your joy may be full.

JOHN 15:10–11

AT MY FIRST regular church job I sat behind the organ console where I could reach the piano, choir, or music director without distracting the congregation. As a full-time student, I appreciated this arrangement because I was usually tired and, hidden from sight, could rest without being noticed. One Easter morning, I was not only exhausted but starving. Rummaging in my choir folder, I found a flattened piece of candy. I devoured it, but it caught in my throat just as the director signaled for us to rise and sing the "Hallelujah Chorus" from Handel's *Messiah*. I emerged from my hideaway, tears streaming down my face as I muffled a cough. Putting on my best he-is-risen-indeed smile, I mouthed the words and tried to keep the candy from rising in my throat. It looked like I was weeping with joy. The fact that I was choking on stale chocolate was too down-to-earth for this heavenly occasion.

Soon, my forced smile became real, and I had to keep back both coughing and laughter. The "Hallelujah Chorus" is practically synonymous with joy, even for secular listeners, and this ill-fated rendition reminded me that my joy is not dependent on my performance. Interestingly, I came to know joy more deeply through a less jubilant masterpiece. As a young piano student, my teacher had me watch a documentary on Johann Sebastian Bach, the most magnificent worship musician since David (in my opinion).

Halfway through the documentary, a countertenor began singing. While I did not understand the German lyrics, I could feel what his song was about. I fought back tears as the melody plumbed the depths of my heart and, with exquisite beauty, hinted at transcendent heights of grace. Upon looking up a translation of the lyrics, I discovered that the refrain, "Erbarme dich, mein Gott" ("Have mercy, my God!"), represents the cry of Peter's heart after denying Christ. Unlike written commentaries, which focus on exposition, Bach's music works the emotion of the gospel into his hearers' hearts. That aria drove me to tears. It is not a praise chorus, but—by guiding me through godly grief—it produced in me a more resilient joy.

The Favorite Fruit

Of the fruit of the Spirit, joy is the most commonly associated with musical worship. If you survey your church members, you will likely find that they evaluate worship songs based on whether they "make them feel happy" or "are upbeat." I am reminded of the Christian radio station I grew up listening to: "Positive, encouraging, KLove."[1]

Scripture is clear that joy and singing are inextricable; joy inspires singing and singing increases joy. Rejoicing and singing are used almost interchangeably, and the Psalms (Scripture's songbook) are utterly joy-riddled. They specifically mention singing to the Lord in at least sixty-six verses, and about sixty of these present joyful singing as the right response to God's steadfast love. (Again, love is the root of the fruit.) The final psalm climaxes in a cosmic chorus that includes thirteen calls to praise in only six verses and commands the participation of instrumentalists, dancers, and all living things (Ps. 150). This sounds similar to many of our services today, with instruments blasting and refrains calling people to worship—over and over and over.

From the intuitions of churchgoers to the testimony of the Psalms, it is clear that whatever else musical worship is, it should be joyful. But there is more to this "favorite" fruit than we might expect. Martin Luther described music as the "mistress and governess" of emotion, meaning that music can express, enhance, alleviate, or alter our wants and feelings.[2] Haven't we all experienced this? I literally changed my tune when I met my husband, swapping melancholy folk songs for Broadway ballads. Our desires and decisions are constantly mirrored and

1 "Mission, Beliefs & Values," " KLove, accessed October 2, 2024, https://www.klove.com/.

2 Martin Luther, "Preface to Georg Rhau's Symphoniae Iucundae," in *Liturgy and Hymns*, ed. Ulrich S. Leupold; trans. Paul Zeller Strodach, vol. 53, *Luther's Works*, American Edition, ed. Jaroslav Pelikan and Helmut T. Lehmann (Fortress Press, 1965), 323.

motivated by music. Your gym and favorite café play different music because they have different goals for you as a consumer. The gym manager wants you to get in, sweat, and get out, while the café owner wants you to enjoy your latte long enough to purchase another.

Luther viewed this affectional power of music as a gift of grace, a way of fostering "a calm and joyful disposition."[3] More than a gym manager or café owner, we as worship leaders can influence the emotions and desires of our congregations. We can use music to encourage worshipers toward fruitfulness, just like a peppy playlist can motivate a workout or lo-fi beats a second coffee. But we also can do the opposite, a reality we cannot afford to take lightly.

While Luther championed music as a way of working Scripture into singers' hearts, Ulrich Zwingli, another Reformer, took the opposite approach. Although an accomplished musician himself, Zwingli sought to ban music from worship.[4] He was motivated not by a hatred of music but by the desire to focus exclusively on Scripture. It is perhaps wise to be encouraged by Luther and cautioned by Zwingli, thanking God for music's emotional influence while ensuring that our music is coupled with biblical lyrics and does not detract from clear preaching of the word. We must also take care that our music does not merely influence our feelings but increases our fruitfulness. To do this, we must examine the heart behind truly

3 Martin Luther, *Letters II*, ed. Gottfried G. Krodel, vol. 49, *Luther's Works*, American Edition, ed. Jaroslav Pelikan and Helmut T. Lehmann (Fortress Press, 1972), 428.

4 Jeremy S. Begbie, *Resounding Truth: Christian Wisdom in the World of Music*, Engaging Culture (Baker Academic, 2007), 113.

joyful worship, which includes but is not entirely dependent on our emotions.

Our joy is more than a feeling. It is a *person*: our gracious, suffering, victorious Savior.

Con Grazia

Con grazia is a musical instruction meaning "with grace." This is the essence of joy as a fruit of the Spirit. The Greek term translated as "joy" in Galatians 5:22 is *chara*, which shares a root with *charis*, grace.[5] Joy springs from grace, not just etymologically but ontologically. Thus, our singing will be most joyful when we are most attuned to God's grace.

German pastor and martyr Dietrich Bonhoeffer is known for warning against "cheap grace," which is a nominal Christianity that seeks gospel benefits (salvation) without gospel discipleship (sanctification).[6] By contrast, "costly grace" is won by Christ's sacrificial love and bestowed upon his followers as they are united with him in both joy and suffering. Contained within "cheap grace" is the idea of *cheap joy*, which chases gospel benefits such as comfort and happiness without gospel disciplines such as repentance, dying to self, and suffering for Christ. Without discernment, musical worship can easily promote cheap joy by generating pleasant emotions without proclaiming union with Christ.

The parable of the soils provides a jarring picture of cheap joy: "As for what was sown on rocky ground, this is the one who

5 Frederick William Danker, ed., *A Greek-English Lexicon of the New Testament and Other Early Christian Literature*, 3rd ed. (University of Chicago Press, 2000), 1077, 1080.

6 Dietrich Bonhoeffer, *The Cost of Discipleship*, trans. R. H. Fuller (Macmillan, 1948; repr., Simon & Schuster, 1995), 91.

hears the word and *immediately receives it with joy*, yet he has no root in himself, but endures for a while, and when tribulation or persecution arises on account of the word, immediately he falls away" (Matt. 13:20–21).

The word Jesus uses to describe the response of the seeds sown in rocky soil is the same word Paul lists among the fruit of the Spirit: *chara*. But wait, isn't joy *always* a fruit of the Spirit? Not necessarily. Feeling joy in the moment is not automatically proof of the Spirit's working. As Scottish theologian Sinclair Ferguson writes, "Joy without repentance—which may manifest itself in different ways and emotions—does not go down deep enough to have lasting roots."[7] The shallow soil represents one who hears the gospel and is thrilled: "Fire insurance? Great!" But when trials come, his enthusiasm withers. It was cheap and destined to fail, for he rejoiced in the gift without really loving the giver.

By contrast, consider the good soil, which is "the one who hears the word and understands it. He indeed bears fruit and yields, in one case a hundredfold, in another sixty, and in another thirty" (Matt. 13:23). The good soil represents a heart prepared to receive the gospel and bear its fruit.[8] Such a heart is aware of its brokenness and its need to be planted deep in the love of Jesus. Whereas the shallow soil is quick both to rejoice and recant, the good soil is grounded in Christ's costly grace, ready to mature and bear abundant, *abiding* fruit.

7 Sinclair B. Ferguson, *Maturity: Growing Up and Going On in the Christian Life* (Banner of Truth, 2019), 179.

8 Lane T. Dennis and Wayne Grudem, eds., *ESV Study Bible: English Standard Version* (Crossway, 2016), 1848.

As worship leaders, we spend our lives trying to model and inspire joy in our congregations. This is a noble endeavor, but we must take care that we are not pursuing sprouts without soil—fruit without a root. It will prove more fruitful in the long run if we dig into the source and object of our joy: the grace of God in Christ Jesus. We will be prepared to sing with joy when we prioritize singing *con grazia*—with grace.

God's Joy Is Sufficient

> Whoever sings songs to a heavy heart
> is like one who takes off a garment on a cold day,
> and like vinegar on soda. (Prov. 25:20)

This isn't likely to be any worship leader's favorite verse, but doesn't it ring true? Haven't we all lugged heavy hearts to church only to feel worse when we are called to sing joyfully and can barely open our mouths? This proverb highlights an overlooked tendency in our worship: pushing too quickly from grief to joy. This cheapens both, just like vinegar and soda neutralize each other. If true joy depends not on our fluctuating feelings but on the grace of God in Christ, then we can mourn, lament, and repent without guilt-tripping ourselves into premature cheerfulness. Because God's grace is sufficient for our weakness, we can trust that his joy is sufficient in our sorrow (2 Cor. 12:9).

While studying and working in Scotland, I was surprised when my church sang imprecatory and lament psalms during ordinary services. It was the first time I'd seriously considered that songs of suffering could be included in worship. It was a freeing realization! As joyful as the Psalms are, they include around sixty-five psalms of lament.[9] While joy is not the obvious tone of these psalms, it is at work behind the scenes and shines forth in the end.

In my Bible, Psalm 13 bears penciled-in chord symbols because I couldn't resist setting it to music during a strenuous season. It begins with a series of audacious questions as David cries out to God. But in the fifth verse David remembers that God has never failed, so why would he now? As David remembers God's love, he rejoices even before his situation is resolved (13:6). His joy is restored not in spite of lament but through it.

On a grander scale, our highest joy as Christians was won by way of lament. On the cross, Jesus utters and fulfills David's cry of "My God, my God, why have you forsaken me?" (Matt. 27:46). The second half of this verse is not mentioned in the Gospels, but it would likely have been familiar to Jewish witnesses. It reads, "Why are you so far from saving me, from the words of my groaning?" (Ps. 22:1). We know that God heard David, that we are saved in Christ, and that the Spirit intercedes for us in our groanings (Rom. 8:1–11, 26). Who, then, is this psalm describing? None other than Jesus Christ, who "for the joy that was set before him, endured the cross" (Heb. 12:2). The gospel, like a lament psalm, does not skip the agony of the crucifixion but moves through it to the joy of the resurrection.

Biblical lament is not the end but the means—a process of reorientation by which we confess sin, express sorrow, and reflect

9 Rob Brockman, "The Art of Lament," The Gospel Coalition Canada, March 31, 2021, https://ca.thegospelcoalition.org/.

on grace as we trust God to restore our joy. We don't have to be that annoying singer who calls heavy hearts to rejoice. Instead, we can grieve and repent and, remembering God's grace, return to joy.

Restored Rejoicing

Whether we are leaders, volunteers, or participants, we will all face seasons when our worship feels lackluster—when our initial exuberance has worn off and our emotions do not immediately rise to the occasion. In such seasons, we should boldly pray with David, "Restore to me the joy of your salvation, and uphold me with a willing spirit" (Ps. 51:12). At the same time, we must learn to treat rejoicing as a discipline—something we do not only when we feel joy but to restore and reinforce our joy. That said, here are a few practical tips to reinvigorate your rejoicing.

Don't Rush the Process

Creating good music requires practice, intentionality, and overcoming failure. There are no shortcuts. Our worship often imitates our culture of immediacy as we roll into church for our weekly joy fix before riding off to brunch on an emotional high. But turning from sorrow to joy is a process that Jesus likens to birthing a child because it is painful and time-consuming but, ultimately, life-giving (John 16:16–24).

While the goal of musical worship should be rejoicing, we may need to travel by way of repentance. If we ignore songs that deal honestly with sin or grief, what are we celebrating when we sing of rescue and victory? Joyful worship is a process involving examination, correction, and confession. In Psalm 51, David sings through this process. He begs the Lord to let him "hear joy and gladness" once more, but rather than jumping to praise, he spends time detailing and mourning his transgressions. Then he asks God several times to purge him of his sin and to create in him a clean heart. This painful, vulnerable, lengthy process is the way to a deeper and more durable joy.

Don't rush through repentance and reorientation. Don't cheapen your joy.

Rejoice and Repeat

Great musicians are not people who sometimes enjoy music but people who habitually *make* music. Similarly, the most joyful Christians are those who routinely rejoice. First Peter 1:8 describes believers who "rejoice with joy that is inexpressible and filled with glory." This sounds redundant in English, but it indicates that joy is not just something we feel but something we do. We gather to engage in rejoicing; experiencing joy is secondary.

While Scripture warns against thoughtless or premature celebration, I've found that not singing is more often due to stubbornness than sensitivity. Every church has people who dislike its music and will make their displeasure apparent. As a recovering worship grouch, I promise that participating even in music you don't like will generate more joy.[10]

Rejoicing must also be a rhythm in our daily lives. Just as poor performances tend to result from deficient practice, struggling to

10 See Ryanne Molinari, "Three Reasons You Don't Feel Joyful During Musical Worship," *Ryanne Molinari* (blog), July 26, 2023, https://ryannemolinari.com/.

sing joyfully on Sundays may expose a lack of rejoicing throughout the week. As Bonhoeffer writes, "The more we sing, the more joy we will derive from it."[11] It turns out that the way we express joy (singing) is also the way to cultivate it. When we incorporate singing into our daily routines, we will rejoice more readily in our weekly services.

Reject Comparison

I know a former orchestra conductor who remains infectiously joyful, not because he is the best in his field (although he was world-class) but because he delights in the excellence of other artists. When we compare our voice to another's, envy the resources of a bigger church, or speak bitterly about other musicians, why would we expect to feel joyful?

"Comparison is a thief of joy," the familiar saying goes.[12] This is because comparison is a thief of grace. Bonhoeffer writes, "Self-justification and judging others go together, as justification by grace and serving others go together."[13] Because comparison is an attempt to justify ourselves over and against others—rather than embracing justification by grace—it is no wonder that it poisons our joy. Far from comparing ourselves to others, God's grace requires us to rejoice in them. This is what we see in Paul, who refers to the Philippians as his "joy and crown" (Phil. 4:1).[14]

11 Dietrich Bonhoeffer, *Life Together: The Classic Exploration of Christian Community*, trans. John W. Doberstein (HarperOne, 1954), 61.

12 Commonly attributed to Theodore Roosevelt.

13 Bonhoeffer, *Cost of Discipleship*, 91.

14 Sam Crabtree, *Practicing Affirmation: God-Centered Praise of Those Who Are Not God* (Crossway, 2011), 76.

Rejecting comparison protects our joy because it frees us to notice God's grace at work in ourselves and others.

Praise Without Ceasing

The best musicians are great noticers. No phrase is unimportant, no detail is too small. No part of life is separate from their creative work or beyond the scope of their imagination. In the same way, joyful people tend to be attentive people. They make a habit of noticing and marveling at God's grace in his word and world.

Scripture tells us to "rejoice always" and "pray without ceasing" (1 Thess. 5:16–17). These are tall orders, but constant rejoicing and prayer can be combined in habitual praise. Blessing God in all things was a common Jewish practice at the time of Jesus and one we can learn much from today. This can be as simple as thanking God throughout the day for anything and everything we find noteworthy or praiseworthy (see Phil. 4:8). Praise God for a steaming cup of tea in the church foyer. Praise God for a singer who practiced diligently before rehearsal. Praise God for a new volunteer with a wealth of experience. Praise God for a perfectly tuned guitar. Praise God for beautiful lyrics, well-timed cymbals, and clapping congregations.

Practice praise, and joy will follow.

Consider Simplifying Your Services

We instinctively seem to equate "joyful" worship with addition—more production value, amplified volumes, faster tempos. But occasionally simplifying our services can help us return to the root of joy. Hebrews describes Christians who "joyfully accepted the plundering of [their] property." How many of us would be-grudgingly allow our property to be stolen—let alone joyfully? But these believers were prepared to rejoice in their loss because they had "a better possession and an abiding one" in Christ (Heb. 10:34). They were not dependent on more, more, more because they had everything in Christ. Including simpler services now and then can guard against relying on certain musical or technical elements to *feel* joy and, instead, help us focus on Christ, our joy.

Closing Hymn: "O Love That Will Not Let Me Go"

Scottish preacher George Matheson (1842–1906) was born with severely limited eyesight. Still, he excelled in academics and went on to serve as a respected minister, lecturer, and writer. Despite the extreme challenges posed by his near blindness, Matheson never lost sight of God's grace. He remained determinedly joyful in the face of tremendous loss and loneliness.[15]

On the evening of his closest sister's wedding, keenly aware of his solitude and battling "extreme mental distress," Matheson scribbled the poem he is best remembered for: "O Love That Will Not Let Me Go." He described this hymn as "the fruit of pain" but said that writing it felt like transcribing someone else's words.[16] In a way, this is accurate: The words of this hymn spill over from Scripture, which Matheson memorized with fervor and

15 Josh Weidmann, "The Blind Preacher Who Saw Quite Well: A Short Bio of George Matheson," *Josh Weidmann* (blog), accessed October 2, 2024, https://joshweidmann.com/.

16 John Julian, *A Dictionary of Hymnology* (Dover, 1907), 2:1579, 1583–84.

depth. In his time of need, he was able to recall these promises and trust God not only to sustain him through loneliness and grief but to restore his joy.

O love that will not let me go,
I rest my weary soul in thee;
I give thee back the life I owe,
That in thine ocean depths its flow
May richer, fuller be.

O Light that follows all my way,
I yield my flick'ring torch to thee;
My heart restores its borrowed ray,
That in thy sunshine's blaze its day
May brighter, fairer be.

O Joy that seekest me thru' pain,
I cannot close my heart to thee;
I trace the rainbow thru' the rain
And feel the promise is not vain
That morn shall tearless be.

O cross that liftest up my head,
I dare not ask to fly from thee;
I lay in dust life's glory dead,
And from the ground there blossoms red
Life that shall endless be.[17]

17 George Matheson, "O Love That Wilt Not Let Me Go," Hymnary.org, 1882, https://hymnary.org/.

Reflection/Discussion

1. How has this chapter changed or challenged your view of joyful worship?

2. Do you find yourself selecting music to reflect or alter your mood? What effect does your favorite music have on your emotional state?

3. Can you think of any worship songs that include elements of lament or confession? Do you sing these in your services?

4. Does your congregation treat joy as a habit? How do you and your church prioritize rejoicing beyond Sunday services?

5. Do you struggle with comparison? How can you replace this with praise?

3

Peace

Embodying Harmony

And let the peace of Christ rule in your hearts, to which indeed you were called in one body. And be thankful.

COLOSSIANS 3:15

CHOOSING AN INTRODUCTION for this chapter was a daunting task—not because I couldn't think of a story to share but because I could think of *dozens*.

I recall the time a choir encircled its audience to sing a beautiful but meaningless song, simulating a sense of peace without any substance. I know of churches that proclaim peace so loudly that they offer earplugs to stave off hearing loss. On the other hand, I've seen disgruntled deacons make a show of measuring decibels and voicing their disapproval.

I am saddened by churches that sing more about society than salvation, proclaiming peace on earth while forgetting heaven. But I am also distraught by those that sing about heaven while failing to promote harmony and wholeness on earth.

I often lament separate services, laughing and cringing over the time a contemporary service attendee asked if I was a visitor, only to discover that I had been the traditional worship director at her church for over a year.

The multiplicity of these competing illustrations suggests how neglected true peace—otherworldly oneness—has become in musical worship. As we try to make music, we too often seem to break peace. We have forgotten the reality so beautifully captured by Bonhoeffer: "It is not you that sings, it is the Church that is singing, and you, as a member of the Church, may share in its song."[1]

The Forgotten Fruit

The word for "peace" in Galatians 5:22 is *eirēnē*. In ancient Greece, *Eirēnē* was a Hora, a minor goddess personifying national stability and prosperity.[2] For Christians, this term became at once more specific and comprehensive. It occurs ninety-two times in the New Testament and refers not merely to earthly tranquility but to salvation in Jesus Christ, the assurance and contentment of Christians, the unity of the church, and the future state of believers in heaven and the new creation.[3] As a Hora, *Eirēnē*

1 Dietrich Bonhoeffer, *Life Together: The Classic Exploration of Christian Community*, trans. John W. Doberstein (HarperOne, 1954), 61.

2 Liana Miate, "Horae," in *World History Encyclopedia*, March 29, 2023, https://www.worldhistory.org/.

3 Joseph H. Thayer, *Thayer's Greek-English Lexicon of the New Testament* (1889; repr., Hendrickson, 2023), 182.

referred to the delicate balance of national security. As a fruit of the Spirit, it refers to kingdom security—the total reconciliation, comfort, well-being, and hope of those who belong to Christ (Luke 1:32–33).

We commonly use the word *peace* to denote comfort and quiet, and it certainly includes these. Like *shalom* in Hebrew, though, *eirēnē* extends farther and deeper. For Christians, it is the eternal rest that comes from being made right with God, the quietness of souls living together in harmony, and the promised comfort of a day when our bodies and souls will be remade in perfect unity. Such peace can be thought of, most simply, as being put back in order or set at one. A good way to think of this is in medical terms: True peace is not just the alleviation of symptoms but a complete cure. For Christians this restoration begins with reconciliation to God in Christ Jesus and is lived out in communion with one another and integrity as whole persons: body and soul.

Unfortunately, if joy is the "favorite" fruit in musical worship, peace seems to be the "forgotten" fruit. As my fragmented introduction illustrates, our singing is too often characterized by fleshly dissonance than by otherworldly harmony. And this is what our peace should be: *otherworldly*. It is "not as the world gives," and it surpasses earthly understanding (John 14:27; Phil. 4:7). Musical worship is not meant to be a breeding ground for strife, jealousy, rivalries, dissension, and division, which are works of the flesh (Gal. 5:20). These destroy our peace, threatening our relationships with God, with one another, and even within ourselves (Rom. 7:15–20). Instead, we must learn to treat musical worship as a means by which the Spirit "sets us at one again." When we gather to sing, we must proclaim the radical reconciliation between God and man, promote unity among Christians, and provide an opportunity for individual worshipers to participate as whole persons.

Vertical Peace

Peaceful worship is cruciform: cross-shaped. It extends vertically as it proclaims reconciliation between God and man and horizontally as it strengthens bonds between Christians.

To construct a cross, the vertical beam must be driven into the ground first. So too, with peace; it must be made vertically before it can extend horizontally. The prerequisite for peace is being right with God. Throughout Scripture, *eirēnē* is inextricable from the gospel, which is good news because it proclaims peace with God in Christ (Luke 1:79; Acts 10:36; Rom. 5:1). That said, if our music generates a sense of calm but avoids clear articulations of the gospel, it is deceitful, perhaps lulling listeners into dangerous complacency. We do not want to become like those described in Jeremiah, "saying, 'Peace, peace,' when there is no peace" (Jer. 6:14). To pursue peace in our worship, we must proclaim the gospel in our songs.

As with joy, peace is about more than our feelings, although it does include them. Just as the best way to experience enduring joy is to focus on the grace of God, the best way to promote peace in our worship is by looking to Christ. Trying to foster peaceful feelings without singing of peace with God in Christ is like trying to fall asleep; the more you think about sleep itself, the more restless you'll become. But if you focus on something else—something that truly brings comfort and security—you are more likely to enjoy a good night's rest. There is nothing wrong with trying to create a restful atmosphere in our worship through mellow music or soothing songs. We should want our services to be a place of respite and for our people to leave refreshed. We cannot offer true peace, however, without singing of our Prince of Peace.

Jesus says, "Blessed are the peacemakers" not "Blessed are the peace*keepers*" (Matt. 5:9). Unlike peacekeeping, peacemaking is not about sitting safely in the status quo, singing music that makes hearers feel comfortable while their souls remain in peril. Instead, our songs must be courageous declarations of our King's peace terms: repentance and faith in Christ Jesus.

Horizontal Harmony

Instructions for orderly worship in 1 Corinthians 14:26 include various saints bringing a hymn to share. If we did this today, I imagine many of us would bring our favorite music not to make peace but to make a point—to prove that our songs are the best songs and our styles the best styles. But Paul is explicit: Whatever song or lesson or revelation or interpretation we bring to worship must be "for building up."

We are often more eager to express our displeasure with certain musical styles than we are "eager to maintain the unity of the Spirit in the bond of peace" (Eph. 4:3). As a fruit of the Spirit (a characteristic of those who are already in Christ), peace refers primarily to the harmony between believers, and "peacemakers" are those who work to establish such harmony.[4] Singing together

4 Frederick William Danker, ed., *A Greek-English Lexicon of the New Testament and Other Early Christian Literature*, 3rd ed. (University of Chicago Press, 2000), 287; hereafter, BDAG.

has the potential to generate interpersonal concord as it reminds us of our shared life in Christ and draws us into a mutual activity. And yet, we often turn it into a medium for contention. We too readily scorn the songs of Christians whose tastes, skills, and experiences differ from ours and devote ourselves to separate services. As secure citizens of the kingdom, why are we so quick to wage civil wars over worship? Why are we so quick to replace harmony with dissonance? Let's consider a few pragmatic steps toward being peacemakers in our approach to musical worship.

First, we need to restrain our tongues from derogatory speech. This does not mean that we stop evaluating the truthfulness of our lyrics or the morality of our leaders, but we must refuse to unfairly denigrate the worship of other Christians. It troubles me that the tongues that speak the most passionately about the need for beautiful music in the church are often prone to speak harsh, ugly things about other worship styles or—worse—other worshipers. Our tongues are double-talkers, alternately blessing God in worship and cursing those who worship appropriately yet differently. As James writes, "My brothers, these things ought not be so" (James 3:9–10).

Worshipers, these things ought not be so.

Second, we need to be open to reason and willing to set aside our preferences. My own failures have taught me that those who have a relatively high musical or theological knowledge tend to be the most divisive in musical worship, readily criticizing leaders or styles who do not reflect their "standards." But James writes that the pure wisdom gained by knowing Christ manifests in being peaceable, open to reason, and impartial (James 3:17–18). Knowledge is good, and I hope worship leaders will study music and theology with enthusiasm, but we must also pursue wisdom. We must learn to listen to and interact with other styles without immediately becoming defensive.

Third, we need to train our tongues to sing, whether or not we like the music. As with joy, it is far better for us to participate in worship together than to sit in stubborn, solitary silence. Worship leaders, we will have to sing or play certain songs over and over because they serve our church members even though they're driving us crazy. Participants, we will have to submit to our leaders by singing the songs they choose without grumbling. In either case, peacemaking is going to take a great deal of personal sacrifice. And yet, our peace with God was won by Christ crucified, so why would we expect peace with one another to demand anything less than dying to ourselves? (Col. 1:19–20).

In my experience, a common "solution" to conflicts over worship music is to host separate services. While I hope diverse worship styles will continue to thrive in the church universal, is dividing our local church bodies like this biblical? Separating based on musical preferences also tends to split congregations based on other factors such as age. But shouldn't we want to hear the voices of children, parents, teenagers, young adults, and grandparents joining together in praise? If Paul refused to allow the Roman Christians to divide over something as serious as whether to eat meat sacrificed to idols, I doubt he would ever advise them to separate over whether to use organs or keyboards, new songs or old hymns (Rom. 14).

Offering services with different worship styles is not overtly wrong, and I've seen that it is possible—with great intentionality and self-awareness—for church members to maintain unity despite attending separate services. And, pragmatically, this approach is not without benefits, such as allowing traditional and contemporary worship to flourish in their own spheres in a way that is not typically feasible in blended services. Still, it is worth asking whether this "solution" lends itself more to peace*keeping* or peace*making*—getting our way or dying to ourselves. It is easy, after all, to get along with people when you do not have to live and worship beside them.

For all its challenges, aren't you glad to live in a world with a variety of musical genres? And don't you look forward to eternity, when we will add our unique voices to the wildly diverse chorus of saints from every nation, tribe, people, language, and era? (Rev. 7:9). I expect we will hear many old psalms and hymns, and Scripture is clear that new songs will be there too (14:3). In the meantime, let's take care not to denounce the songs in which God seems to delight, or to dismiss the singers he deeply loves.

When we commit to making peace by retraining our tongues and setting aside our preferences, we are promised a rich reward. Such sacrificial peacemaking paves the way for further fruitfulness: "a harvest of righteousness" in ourselves and those worshiping with us (James 3:18).

Let's not just be music-makers but peacemakers.

Body and Soul

Eirēnē (like *shalom* in Hebrew) also refers to the total well-being of an individual as both body and soul. We typically talk about the gospel in terms of "saving souls," but its peace is good news for our bodies as well. When Jesus heals a woman with a flow of blood, for example, he addresses her as an entire person, saying, "Daughter, your faith has made you well; go in peace, and be healed of your disease" (Mark 5:34). This woman experiences total peace; her bleeding body is healed by the one who will bleed to save her soul. The peace of Christ includes the restoration of her body, as it will for us when we are raised with him.

Peaceful worship should promote unity in the body of Christ as well as the integrity of each worshiper as an embodied person. We often sing of feeling peace in our souls ("It is well with my *soul*," "Be still, my *soul*"), but singing is an embodied activity. Let's not forget that our "spiritual worship" requires us to present our *bodies* as living sacrifices (Rom. 12:1). When we gather to sing, we have the opportunity to use our bodies fruitfully and to minister to others spiritually and physically.

"If a brother or sister is poorly clothed and lacking in daily food, and one of you says to them, 'Go in peace, be warmed and filled,' without giving them the things needed for the body, what good is that?" (James 2:15–16). If our worship proclaims peace but is heedless of embodiment, it's missing the mark. I fear we sometimes seek more to amplify our gifts than to include worshipers with various disabilities or disorders. For example, a family friend sustained a traumatic brain injury, and while she continues to prioritize in-person worship, she often has to step outside when the volume or effects become too intense.

While dramatic audiovisual effects can be used to God's glory, Scripture is clear that tending to one another's weaknesses must take precedence over exercising our strengths. Flashing lights may create a powerful atmosphere, but they also make it difficult or dangerous for those prone to migraine and epilepsy to participate. Fog machines create an aura of mystery but might hinder those with respiratory issues from singing comfortably. People on the autism spectrum or with other sensory issues may struggle with overstimulating services in general.

Realistically, we cannot be constantly and completely aware of every attendee's physical needs and limitations. We should, however, take care to observe our congregations closely and welcome feedback on this subject. We must be willing to examine our practices and explore accommodations, doing our best not to bar the very people who attracted Jesus so powerfully from corporate worship.

It is also sadly common not just to exclude worshipers with health issues but to unintentionally harm those who are otherwise healthy. I know of a former worship leader who is barely thirty but already suffers severe hearing loss because of the extreme volume of his church's music. (Scripture certainly recommends loud praise, but it is unlikely that the instruments used in biblical times had the deafening power of modern technology.)

If we desire health for our congregations, we as worship leaders must be accountable for ourselves first. We need to tend to our bodies as carefully as we tune our instruments. More so than keyboards and guitars and drums, our bodies are our instruments (Rom. 6:13). In fact, the term translated as "instruments" here refers to tools or even weapons.[5] Our bodies are meant to be exercised, refined, and protected so that they are equipped

5 BDAG 716.

for effective and enduring worship. No soldier would purposely blunt his arrows or chip his sword, and (hopefully) none of us are smashing our guitars on stage, so why would we do anything less than steward our bodies so we can lead as well as possible for as long as possible?

When we care for human embodiment in our worship, we give our congregations a glimpse of when all things will be made right—when we will receive our spiritual bodies and join in the radiant, resounding praise of the resurrection without fear, pain, or inability.

Making Music, Practicing Peace

Although musical worship is often characterized by relational dissonance, I've learned through years of working with church choirs that it can also be an invaluable way of cultivating the core aspects of peace we touched on in this chapter. When we sing together, we practice gospel proclamation, harmony and orderliness, and holistic participation.

Gospel Proclamation

I'll admit it: solo singing is not my forte, but years of singing in and collaborating with choirs has increased my confidence. As we have seen, our job as peacemakers calls us to boldly declare God's terms of peace. Musical worship presents us with an opportunity to practice this proclamation together week after week. When we sing lines such as "I once was blind but now I see," we remember the gospel and rehearse our testimonies.[6] As we sing

6 John Newton, "Amazing Grace! (How Sweet the Sound)," Hymnary.org, 1779 https://hymnary.org/.

gospel-centered songs together, we equip one another with the words and the confidence to go out and share the good news of peace in Christ.

Singing together is also an opportunity to proclaim the gospel through our radical unity. If our songs declare the gospel but our congregations are rife with division, something is clearly amiss. Onlookers will wonder whether the gospel has any power in our lives here and now, or if it is solely about the future state of our souls. Instead, when we choose to sing with unity, the otherworldly oneness of the church becomes what theologian Steven Guthrie describes as "an aural reality."[7] In other words, setting aside the lesser things that threaten to divide us and choosing to sing together renders what the Apostles' Creed calls "the communion of saints" visible *and audible* to the world.

Harmony and Orderliness

For harmony to exist in life—as in music—there must be more than one voice. Interestingly, though, harmony is not total equality. This does not mean that some singers are more valuable than others, but that certain parts must sing softer or louder for the sake of balance. For example, my church choir has more sopranos than basses. If the sopranos and basses sang with equal volume, their music would have an upside-down, top-heavy quality. Instead, my sopranos must temper their singing so they can hear the basses. Then the chords begin to click and the harmonies "shimmer" in a way that they would not if everyone sang the same volume all the time, regardless of harmonic hierarchy.

7 Steven R. Guthrie, *Creator Spirit: The Holy Spirit and the Art of Becoming Human* (Baker Academic, 2011), 80.

Harmony in our worship affirms the equal dignity of all Christians but requires orderliness. Harmony is not every team member singing or playing full force. It is not every congregation member voicing his or her opinions with equal weight. Rather, it is learning when it is appropriate to lead and when to follow—musically and organizationally.

Leaders, like the basses in a choir, you set the tone for your church's singing. Laypeople—like sopranos in a church choir—you outnumber your leaders, but it's your job to tune to them, sharing your insight peaceably and being willing to adjust. As in music, it is not identicality and uniformity that makes for harmony, but different saints submitting to one another in a clear and peaceful order (1 Cor. 14:26–33; Eph. 5:19–21).

Holistic Participation

After the COVID-19 pandemic, I was tasked with relaunching a church choir. While the members were all skilled musicians, singing as an ensemble after years apart required more than individual musical ability. We had to work on technique and warm-ups, rebuilding vocal strength and physical stamina. Singers also had to learn vulnerability, being willing to sing expressively without fear of embarrassment. We worked on aligning vowels and consonants so our lyrics would be clear despite being sung by multiple voices. Through all of this, we also shared prayer requests and life updates. Far from being tangential, this fellowship is essential to musical harmony; as singers grow in relationship, they learn to sing *with* one another rather than simply *beside* one another.

Singing is a whole-person activity. We know that it is spiritual, but it is also physical, emotional, intellectual, and relational. It engages our spirits, hearts, and minds, and shapes the way we interact with one another. Does this sound familiar? I'm reminded of the greatest commandment, to "love the Lord your God with all your heart and with all your soul and with all your strength and with all your mind, and your neighbor as yourself" (Luke 10:27). Musical worship is an opportunity to practice this greatest commandment—to foster godly love while we pursue holistic peace.

When we gather to worship, we bring our whole selves to the table: heart, soul, strength, and mind. We also prepare to worship the Lord with our neighbors—those singing beside us. We join together physically as we stand and breathe as one, emotionally as we participate in songs of praise and lament, intellectually as we focus on the same text, and, of course, spiritually as we worship the same Lord in the same Spirit. Just as regular rehearsals can transpose a group of singers into a choir and then turn choir membership into genuine friendship, musical worship can help us appreciate the way God crafted us as whole persons—soul, mind, heart, and strength—and can propel us into deeper relationship with one another.

Closing Hymn: "How Can I Keep from Singing?"

Shalom is a way of bidding one another hello and goodbye, of wishing one another total well-being in meeting and parting. How fitting, then, to conclude this chapter with a song that conveys peace both musically and lyrically. Typically sung at a relaxed tempo with minimal accompaniment, this hymn creates a calm and restful atmosphere. Its verses point toward the total restoration we will experience in the new creation and remind us that, even now, we can experience glimmers of this peace by persisting in praise.

As the refrain of this song emphasizes, our peace is rooted in Christ. Truly, with such a Savior, how can we keep from singing—regardless of the song or style?

My life flows on in endless song,
Above earth's lamentation.
I catch the sweet, though far-off hymn
That hails a new creation.

[Refrain] No storm can shake my inmost calm
While to that Rock I'm clinging.
Since Christ is Lord of heav'n and earth,
How can I keep from singing?

Through all the tumult and the strife,
I hear that music ringing.
It finds an echo in my soul.
How can I keep from singing?

What though my joys and comforts die,
I know my Savior liveth.
What though the darkness gather round?
Songs in the night he giveth.

The peace of Christ makes fresh my heart,
A fountain ever springing!
All things are mine since I am his!
How can I keep from singing?[8]

8 "How Can I Keep from Singing?," Hymnary.org. Author and date unknown.

Discussion/Reflection

1. Do you agree that musical worship is often a source of division among Christians? Have you experienced this?

2. Jesus says his peace is not of this world (John 14:27). In what ways is your church's musical worship otherworldly?

3. Much of our worship music focuses on vertical peace between man and God. Does your church also sing songs that encourage horizontal peace between Christians?

4. How do you tend to think and talk about other worship styles? Spend some time this week exploring a different genre of worship music than you are used to, perhaps attending another service or listening to another leader's setlist.

5. Think about the last service you led or attended. Consider how it engaged (or neglected) the following:

   a. Heart (emotions/will)

   b. Mind (intellect/rationality)

   c. Soul (faith/belief)

   d. Strength (body/physicality)

   e. Neighbor (relationships/community)

4

Patience

Rehearsing for Eternity

Put on then, as God's chosen ones, holy and beloved, compassionate hearts, kindness, humility, meekness, and patience, bearing with one another and, if one has a complaint against another, forgiving each other; as the Lord has forgiven you, so you also must forgive.

COLOSSIANS 3:12–13

MY FIRST SUNDAY leading worship as a graduate student in St. Andrews, Scotland, is burned into my memory. I was determined not to miss any cues, keenly conscious that I (a nondenominational pianist) was punching beyond my weight—thrust suddenly onto the organ bench of a historic Scottish congregation. The sense of ceremony—with blood-red robes, solemn processionals, and the liturgy read in glorious accents—was awe-inspiring, and I was eager to do my part with excellence.

Too eager.

As soon as I finished my prelude, I pulled out all the stops and launched into the opening hymn before I could second-guess myself.

I should have second-guessed.

It would have given the presiding elder time to start announcements. Instead, I played in ignorant bliss while the poor gentleman kept calm and carried on. Finally realizing he could not compete with the volume of a pipe organ on full blast, he and a few others joined not in singing but shouting. After a few more measures, I realized that they were not shouting for some pleasant reason like the church being on fire. They were shouting for me to stop.

My eagerness's evil twin, impatience, had reared its ugly head. Determined to avoid awkward silences, I created an awkward cacophony as I played over announcements. My face redder than my robe, I stopped playing. "Typical American," I berated myself, "always loud and rushing about." I am thankful that this congregation and, in particular, my organ teacher remained patient with me as I learned the rhythms of their worship. Because they were committed to my development as a church musician, they were willing to bear with a few growing pains along the way.

While starting a hymn too swiftly is far from sinful, this incident revealed something unfruitful in me: a desire to always be moving forward, seeking immediate gratification and constant stimulation in worship as in life. Patience, however, invites us to wait on the Lord and to endure alongside one another as we rehearse for a chorus even better than the most beautiful Anglican anthems: the eternal refrain of "Holy, Holy, Holy."

The Forbearing Fruit

The word for "patience" in Galatians 5:22 (*makrothumia*) is a compound of *makros* (long in distance or time) and *thumos* (passion, such as indignation or wrath).[1] A more literal translation is "longsuffering" (KJV; ASV). Patience is about restraint, keeping our annoyance, anger, and even ambition in check.[2] It is about resisting immediacy and investing in relationships. It is about learning when to be still and silent for the sake of sanctification. Patience is about playing the long game, becoming more like Christ and preparing one another for an eternity of praise.

Another Greek word translated as patience (*hupomonē*) refers to enduring difficult circumstances. While this is not the sort of patience listed among the fruit of the Spirit, it is a related concept and extremely relevant to musical worship. Both types of patience appear together in Colossians, which exhorts Christians to be strengthened "for all endurance and patience" (Col. 1:11). Anglican theologian R. C. Trench explains that "*makrothymia* refers to patience with respect to persons, *hypomonē* with respect to things."[3] *Makrothumia* is thus an attribute of God, who bears with rebellious man—allowing time for us to repent, be saved,

1 Frederick William Danker, ed., *A Greek-English Lexicon of the New Testament and Other Early Christian Literature*, 3rd ed. (University of Chicago Press, 2000), 461, 612 ; hereafter, BDAG.

2 Joseph H. Thayer, *Thayer's Greek-English Lexicon of the New Testament* (1889; repr., Hendrickson, 2023), 386.

3 R. C. Trench, *Trench's Synonyms of the New Testament*, ed. Robert G. Hoerber, et al. (Baker, 1989), 209.

and honor him through transformed lives (Rom. 2:4). Likewise, patience as a fruit of the Spirit is relational and redemptive. It calls us to endure alongside one another and, often, to endure one another.

Paul writes, "But I received mercy for this reason, that in me, as the foremost, Jesus Christ might display his perfect patience as an example to those who were to believe in him for eternal life" (1 Tim. 1:16). Jesus bore with Paul as he persecuted the early church, finally appearing to him and asking, "Why are you persecuting me?" (Acts 9:4). As his people suffer, Jesus suffers. And yet, he mercifully waits. He will return and execute justice in the fullness of time, but now, in the in-between, he *suffers long* so that many might turn to him (2 Pet. 3:9–10).

Patience invites us to represent Christ to one another, bearing with one another's weaknesses and waiting on the Lord in both song and silence. You can probably think of many such patience-demanding situations: a practice session where your hands or voice would not cooperate, a rehearsal where several musicians forgot their music or sent last-minute excuses for not coming, or a service when the volunteer running slides was consistently behind. Leading worship, as it combines music-making and relationship-building, presents us with manifold opportunities for practicing patience—for persevering in our craft and alongside one another.

Spiritual Maturity Over Musical Mastery

While studying in the United Kingdom, I became aware of an odd phenomenon: awarding church scholarships to outspokenly non-Christian students. I had naively assumed that I was offered an organ scholarship because I was a Christian first and a musician second. And yet, it became evident that musical aptitude was the scholarship's sole standard. Saving faith in Jesus Christ was not part of the job description, although it was a happy bonus.

Upon returning to the United States, I found that my eyes had been opened. Everywhere I turned, I saw even biblically conservative churches hiring nonbelieving musicians to help lead worship. One such church was nearly four thousand attendees strong. Could they really not find a competent Christian cellist among this multitude? Or had the expediency of hiring a professional been too appealing? It is much more efficient to work with performers who can waltz in for a sound check and play a note-perfect service than to provide opportunities to volunteers who may require extra coaching. Such shortcuts create pleasant experiences for attendees and stress-free rehearsals for leaders, but they come at a cost beyond mere hiring fees. Are we really willing to exchange the edification of musicians in our congregations for the entertainment value and ease of hiring non-Christians?

More to the point, are we really willing to prioritize musical expediency over the worship that most delights God—worship that is "a *sacrifice* of praise" and "the fruit of lips that *acknowledge his name*" (Heb. 13:15)? Committing to exclusively Christian worship is a sacrifice; it will demand immense patience.

I rejoice whenever a trained musician joins my choir, but my fundamental concern is that anyone leading or serving under my direction is a professing Christian first and a proficient musician second. As simple as this principle sounds, it is difficult to uphold. It makes it harder to find someone to fill in for me when I am away, which means fewer vacations. It is more challenging to select repertoire for my ensemble since I have to manage the varying abilities and availability of volunteers versus the predictability of professionals. But these difficulties are teaching me patience and, as the years progress, I am rewarded by seeing those in my ministry develop musically and spiritually.

I know how tough it is to find reliable work as a musician, and churches often represent sanctuaries for struggling artists—stable side jobs that provide financial (if not spiritual) salvation. Hiring nonbelievers often comes from a good desire to provide work for artists in our communities and, perhaps, to usher them into the faith. But let me put this bluntly: Inviting non-Christians to lead the bride of Christ in song is not only impatient; it is deceptive.

I would hire some of my non-Christian musician friends in a heartbeat for other gigs but putting them before my congregation would be an inauthentic representation of who we are as the church. Such a decision fails to serve either group. It indicates to non-Christian professionals that they are fine just as they are and to Christian volunteers that their service is unwanted. It reveals that our view of musical worship places greater value on music than on worship. It suggests that we are more concerned with curating a flawless experience that demands little from us than we are about creating opportunities for Christians to *address one another* in singing (Eph. 5:19).

While the warning against being "unequally yoked" is typically thought of in terms of marriage between believers and nonbelievers, the principle rings true in our worship as well. "What accord has Christ with Belial? Or what portion does a believer share with an unbeliever? What agreement has the temple of God with idols?

For we are the temple of the living God" (2 Cor. 6:15–16). What business do goats—however talented—have in leading sheep?

It is impatient to skip over volunteer or amateur Christians in favor of nonbelieving professionals. If we are unwilling to bear with our musical brothers and sisters—to "suffer long" as they learn to lead—how can we expect to bear with them through actual trials? We must prioritize spiritual maturity over musical mastery, the profession of Christ over music as a profession.

It can be discouraging to feel that we must choose between perseverance and precision or between authenticity and aesthetics, but when we resolve to seek out and champion the gifts of other Christians, we will likely be surprised at the talents buried in our churches that are waiting to be discovered and developed. Finding and training Christian musicians will require more time and energy, but it is a matchless opportunity for cultivating patience in ourselves, our teams, and our churches. Even as we continue to pursue musical excellence, we must remember that our goal is virtue, not virtuosity and fruitful people, not flawless performances.

Sanctification Over Stimulation

Recently, while practicing, I noticed that I was playing the notes but not the rests. I kept skipping them in favor of rapid scales, treacherous arpeggios, and intricate ornamentations. Why waste time on the rests? Who needs to practice *not* playing the piano?

But not playing is part of playing, just as patience requires restraint as well as action. It's important to practice rests because, without them, our sense of rhythm falls apart and our listeners have no time to let the music sink in. I have found that skipping musical rests is symptomatic of my general lack of patience. I tend to prefer sound over silence and stimulation over the slowly evolving beauty of a piece of music or an unhurried worship service.

Another meaning of *makrothumia* is "a state of remaining tranquil while awaiting an outcome."[4] When you think about it, it makes sense that stillness and silence would be connected with patience. When do we most need to be patient? When we are waiting for something that has not yet arrived. When we are living and worshiping in the "in-between"—embracing salvation in Christ while anticipating his return and navigating messy relationships as redeemed people.

Psalm 62:5 reads, "For God alone, O my soul, wait in silence, for my hope is from him." Waiting on God in silence is a prerequisite for patience. It is not comfortable, but it is good, like well-timed rests in a piece of music that render the notes all the more striking. The "forbearing fruit" ripens in stillness. In our worship, we do not need to constantly smooth over quiet moments with more music or rush from song to song. When we feel compelled to play faster, louder, or more, we should consider whether we are seeking to promote endurance or struggling to keep people (ourselves included) entertained.

I was made aware of this tension between stimulation and sanctification during my first few weeks in Scotland. I noticed that the music director at my church would play the Communion hymns and then let the congregation receive the bread and wine in silence—well, not exactly silence. The scuffling, snuffling noises of a group of people trying hard to move quietly echoed in the stone

4 BDAG 612.

sanctuary. I confess, such "silence" tests my patience, as a magnet on my refrigerator attests. It declares in bolded capitals, "I am not emotionally equipped to deal with the sound of someone chewing." It's much easier to *feel* patient when there's music obscuring the slurping of my neighbor as she takes the cup, the fussing of infants as they are blessed, or the creaking of joints as they kneel. When it was my turn to play for service, I resolved to improvise during Communion to conceal the aggravating sounds of human existence—chewing being the foremost.

Before I could carry out my plan, a choir member seemed to read my mind and told me to wait. "It's good to give everyone, including yourself, a moment to breathe," she said.

So I did—or, rather, did not. I sat with my hands folded and worried that others felt the same discomfort I did. Were they inwardly blaming me for not doing anything? For forcing them to hear each other's movements? Eventually, I came to welcome this stillness as "salutary," to borrow the liturgical word for something that is spiritually curative even if it is not initially comfortable.

If I must drown out the sounds of others as they partake of the Lord's Supper, what chance do I have of suffering alongside them in life beyond Sunday services? If I am, as my magnet proclaims, not emotionally equipped to bear with their chewing, how can I aspire to bear with them through failure, weakness, grief, and need? Bearing with others when they are burdensome (or just plain bothersome) is foundational to any real fellowship. Truly, "it is only when he is a burden that another person is really a brother and not merely an object to be manipulated."[5]

5 Dietrich Bonhoeffer, *Life Together: The Classic Exploration of Christian Community*, trans. John W. Doberstein (HarperOne, 1954), 100.

Patience relies on restraint. We must refuse to retaliate when we are wronged or—on a smaller scale—to snap at or bail on others when they annoy us. For this type of patience to exist, we have to remain in community with one another. While physical proximity in our services is a necessary start, it is not enough on its own. Even as we stand beside one another in worship, we may be secretly relieved that the movement and music of our services shield us from actually having to hear or interact with each other.

As worship leaders, we tend to think of our roles in terms of sound: its volume and speed, transitions between songs, buildups to a key change. We are, understandably, concerned with keeping participants engaged and the service flowing. But just as we control the sound in our services, we also control the silence. We ought to reconsider our roles accordingly, learning to treat moments of silence as we would rests in well-written music—not skipping over them but letting them replace instant gratification and constant stimulation with patient sanctification.

Enduring Toward Eternity

The word *patience* is used twenty times in the ESV New Testament. Most of these occurrences are between the Gospels and Revelation—i.e., after Jesus's earthly ministry and before his return. If we were to chart these occurrences on a plot arc, most of them would fall after the climax but before the resolution of the story. This makes sense. Patience is about persevering in the in-between. It is about living together as redeemed people in a broken world—grounded in the gospel and looking toward eternity as we navigate this messy middle.

This in-between life of ours is prime patience season. In fact, this may be the only time we have for cultivating patience. Like music moving through time toward a final cadence, patience propels us toward eternity. There, we will no longer need to "suffer long." There will be no sin or suffering (although with all the feasting, I fear there may still be loud chewing). There, in the absence of sins such as pride, wrath, and sloth, we will no longer have to grit our teeth and bear with each other. Instead, we will open our mouths to rejoice in and with one another (1 Cor. 12:26).

Take heart, worship leader. Doubtless, you have wondered after a grueling rehearsal whether it's really worth it. Does anyone care if the new drummer is a bit behind the beat? Or if a vocalist is turning her harmonies into a solo? Why not give up and give in? Let the band play whatever and however they like. Why spend more time rehearsing than actually singing in service? Why not just hire professionals or lead by yourself? Does worship leading have to take this much patience?

Our ultimate goal surpasses our fleeting rehearsals and services. Just as God is patient with sinners so that they will repent and be saved, so we bear with one another—because as we prepare music for worship, we are also preparing our hearts and relationships for eternity. To persevere through all the long, demanding details of leading worship, we must look ahead to when patience will give way to praise as our gifts and strengths at last merge in seamless harmony.

Music and *Makrothumia*

There can be no doubt that musical worship demands patience. But this is good news: Even beyond worship leading, learning and rehearsing music produces endurance and forbearance. Below are a few final reflections on the relationship between making music and practicing patience.

Practice Makes Patient

While preparing for one of my college recitals, I seemed to live and breathe piano. I began figuring out chord progressions in my sleep, which was helpful (if not restful). Even now, I can see the lime green walls of my favorite practice room when I close my eyes. After my recital, I calculated that I'd spent seven hundred hours mastering a twenty-minute piece, which, fittingly, was based on Dante's *Inferno*.

Seven hundred lonely, exhausting hours, all for twenty measly minutes.

Fortunately, this disciplined practice produced something far more permanent than any performance. Despite the familiar saying, practice does not make perfect. It does, however, make us patient. Chipping away at the same music for months has two possible results: Grow patient or give up. Any accomplished musician you meet is either an extraordinary prodigy or extraordinarily persistent. Given estimates that only one in five to ten million children are prodigies, it's safe to assume that most good musicians are not endowed with genius but have endured years of practice.

Persevere in praise. Keep preparing for and attending services. Let these practices equip you to endure.

Collaboration Demands Patience

My solitary practice hours made me look forward to rehearsals all the more. I welcomed the chance to make music with other people rather than the spiders in the corner of my practice room (with whom

I grew too familiar). Many musicians excel as soloists, but I believe that great artists must also be able to collaborate. While we are called to endure as individuals, patience as a fruit of the Spirit cannot be achieved in isolation. After all, it's pretty easy to bear with people when there are no people, but that's not patience—that's just absence.

While practicing requires us to heed our strengths and weaknesses as musicians, rehearsing forces us to reckon with those of others. Unless you're the director of the Berlin Philharmonic or the Choir of King's College, Cambridge, you know that rehearsals tend to be simultaneously refreshing and frustrating. If a novice comes without practicing or a pro insists on flexing his expertise, the entire group will suffer. In the secular industry, unprepared or disruptive people can be fired. On a volunteer worship team . . . not so much. At least, not as easily.

We as worship leaders must manage wildly diverse skill sets and commitment levels. We may need to position loud singers with questionable pitch beside those who sing quietly but in tune, for instance. Or we may need to schedule extra rehearsals, sacrificing our time to coach volunteers or accommodate their schedules. Coordinating and collaborating is going to teach us patience, whether we like it or not.

But it's not just that others demand our patience; we also require theirs. Even if we are in positions of leadership, it's wise to recognize the ways our teams and congregations bear with *us*. It also helps to reflect and give thanks for the leaders and teachers who did not give up on us as we learned to serve in worship.

Shared Goals Motivate Patience

All this talk of forbearance sounds dismal at best. After all, people often joke about not praying for patience. Why? Because patience is developed via patience-testing situations and relationships. While we desire to possess patience, we are not often eager to practice it.

Thankfully, even as music-making requires us to practice patience, it also reinforces and rewards it. I've worked with choirs composed of singers whose personalities and opinions initially seemed incompatible. But as they sang, their divisions began to dissipate. Intent on a common goal—making beautiful music—they were forced to listen and adjust to one another's tuning, tempo, and tone.

It is no coincidence that some of the strongest communities I've seen in and beyond the church are choirs. If a shared commitment to music-making helps even non-Christians bear with one another, how much more so should a commitment to worship promote patience in our churches?

We've spent most of this chapter talking about bearing with one another, but the way we accomplish this is by paying attention to someone infinitely better than any one of us: our forbearing, forgiving Lord. We shouldn't show up to rehearsals or services bound and determined to tolerate a particular person. If this is our approach, we are already doomed. Instead, we must each focus on our common goal: adoring and emulating Christ. Only then will patience become not only bearable but beautiful.

Closing Hymn: "Be Still, My Soul"

From its opening line, "Be Still, My Soul" softly commands patience. It is generally sung without hurry, allowing singers to grow comfortable with its slow, steady progression from trials and strife to comfort and communion. This hymn includes both types of patience as it describes enduring difficult situations and the loss of beloved friends. It concludes by looking toward eternity, when suffering will be undone and our patience will achieve its perfect end.

Be still, my soul! the Lord is on your side;
Bear patiently the cross of grief or pain;
Leave to your God to order and provide;
In ev'ry change he faithful will remain.
Be still, my soul! your best, your heav'nly friend,
Thru' thorny ways leads to a joyful end.

Be still, my soul! your God doth undertake
To guide the future as he has the past;
Your hope, your confidence, let nothing shake;
All now mysterious shall be bright at last.
Be still, my soul! the waves and winds still know
His voice who ruled them while he lived below.

Be still, my soul! when dearest friends depart
And all is darkened in the vale of tears,
Then shall you better know his love, his heart;
Who comes to soothe your sorrow and your fears.
Be still, my soul! your Jesus can repay
From his own fullness all he takes away.

Be still, my soul! the hour is hast'ning on
When we shall be forever with the Lord,
When disappointment, grief, and fear are gone,

Sorrow forgot, love's purest joys restored.
Be still, my soul! when change and tears are past,
All safe and blessed, we shall meet at last.[6]

Reflection/Discussion

1. Have you ever hired a non-Christian to assist with musical worship? What was your rationale for doing so?

2. Do you find yourself striving to eliminate silence? How can you protect intentional stillness in your life? In your worship?

3. Do you agree with the statement "practice makes patient"? What has practicing music or participating in worship regularly taught you about forbearance and endurance?

4. What conflicts or frustrations are you facing in your ministry or participation? How can focusing on Christ help you deal patiently with others?

5. List at least five ways others have had to bear with you, whether as a leader, student, volunteer, or fellow worshiper. If appropriate, thank these people for their patience.

6 Kathrina von Schlegel, "Be Still, My Soul," trans. Jane Borthwick, Hymnary.org, 1752, https://hymnary.org/.

5

Kindness

Tuning to Usefulness

Note then the kindness and the severity of God: severity toward those who have fallen, but God's kindness to you, provided you continue in his kindness. Otherwise you too will be cut off.

ROMANS 11:22

THE NICEST PLACE I ever worked was not kind.

I spent a few years working as an accompanist at a local college. I was thankful for the job but constantly frustrated—not because the work culture was negative but because it was so deceptively *positive*. All applicants were admitted and applauded, regardless of whether they attended rehearsals, practiced their music, respected their professors, or demonstrated any musical aptitude. Students who could hardly carry a tune were encouraged to enroll and perform as music majors. Rather than sparing these students their time, money, and dignity, faculty cheered them on whether or not they were making responsible, realistic decisions. This approach set up unaware students for humiliation and set back their more capable peers. It was cruelty masquerading as niceness.

Kindness demands honesty.

On the other hand, brutal criticism is not kind either. A piano professor of mine used to share about her years at one of the world's most renowned conservatories. She was under constant stress, and the competition was so fierce that she feared for her safety. She learned from this opposite extreme, training her students with compassion without lowering her standards of excellence.

Kindness is neither superficial politeness nor unrelenting pressure; it calls us to discern and meet the real needs of others, whether this means sharing tough truths or well-timed praise.

The Friendship Fruit

Those who console me in sorrow and celebrate with me in success are my friends. Those who console, celebrate, *and correct* me are my best friends. Like friendship, kindness requires grace and truth.

The word translated as "kindness" in Galatians 5:22 is *chrēstotēs*. Defining this word is tricky because it is inextricable from two other fruits of the Spirit: gentleness and goodness. Our culture correctly assumes that kindness involves courtesy but, like goodness, it also refers to excellence and integrity.[1] So what is kindness?

1 Frederick William Danker, ed., *A Greek-English Lexicon of the New Testament and Other Early Christian Literature*, 3rd ed. (University of Chicago Press, 2000), 1090; hereafter, BDAG.

Is it the soft touch of gentleness or the more rigid standards of goodness?

Perhaps the most succinct and practical way to understand kindness as a fruit of the Spirit is as *usefulness*. It is not so cruelly critical that it destroys relationships, but it is also not so sickly sweet that it destroys lives. It is genuinely helpful and beneficial.[2] Paul uses a related word, *euchrēstos*, to describe the result of Christian obedience: "He will be a vessel for honorable use, set apart as holy, *useful* to the master of the house, ready for every good work" (2 Tim. 2:21).

Kindness is an attribute of God (Rom. 2:4). As with patience, God's kindness is inextricable from his severity. It does not leave us as we are but leads us to repentance and salvation (11:22). Even for Christians, God's kindness involves discipline as he refines us and makes us a holy people (Heb. 12:6, 10). Likewise, kindness compels us to help others live into their redeemed identities. It leads us to offer correction, redirection, and encouragement as we guide our people to use their gifts and serve where they are most effective. It calls us to treat one another as true friends—building one another up and easing one another's burdens through honesty and honor.

"My Yoke Is Kind"

Murals in my city call residents to "Be Kind," and popular T-shirts declare that "Kindness Costs Nothing." While appealing on the surface, these maxims fail to define kindness, leaving us to interpret it as superficial politeness at best and

2 BDAG 1090.

dangerous affirmation at worst. Churches are often tempted by the same mindset, prioritizing niceness over truthfulness. Or, as a reaction against this tendency, Christians may excuse hurtful sarcasm or criticism as "just speaking the truth." But Scripture is clear that kindness requires both tact and truth. Further, kindness *is* costly. God's kindness to us cost him his Son, and genuine kindness may cost us our comfort and pride (Eph. 2:4–7). Our model for this nuanced kindness—this true friendship—is none other than Jesus Christ, who is "full of grace and truth" (John 1:14).

When Jesus describes what it is like to follow him, he employs the root of *chrēstotēs*, *chrēstos*: "For my yoke is easy [*chrēstos*], and my burden is light" (Matt. 11:30). The image of a yoke is lost on many of us today. If we think about yokes at all, we think of them as heavy and constricting, something oxen bear begrudgingly and humans ought to avoid. But yokes were intended to *ease* the discomfort of heavy loads. They did not eliminate burdens but made them manageable by distributing their weight between two animals.[3]

The "yoke" is also a metaphor for the obligations of law or servitude. By fulfilling the Mosaic law, Jesus took upon himself a burden we could not carry. But as animals continue to plow a field, we still must move forward as we serve Christ and one another. And yet we do so with newfound lightness. Following Jesus is not "easy" in the sense of mindlessness or laziness, but in the sense that he bears us up and beckons us forward. He is right beside us, lifting the weight we could not carry and leading us onward.

3 G. J. Wenham, et al., eds., *Matthew*, New Bible Commentary (InterVarsity Press, 1994), 918, Accordance.

In the words of English theologian Jeremy Taylor, "Christ's yoke is like feathers to a bird; not loads, but helps to motion."[4]

This is what kind musical worship ought to be: *a help to motion.* It should propel us forward, encouraging us as we follow Christ and become more like him. This is not always "easy." Like a yoke, leading and gathering for worship is an obligation. At the same time, it should ease our burdens. Our lyrics should offer relief from a world of dishonesty and flattery by proclaiming the truth *in love.* Songs of confession should help us throw off the weight of sin and shame. Songs of forgiveness and assurance should lighten the load of discouragement. And as our voices intermingle and we stand side by side, our musical worship should remind us that we are not alone. Singing together is a visual and aural image of what it means to be in Christ as we carry one another's burdens and press on together.

Kindness Demands Honesty

Almost all terrible performances can be prevented by kindness. Look up a compilation of bad *American Idol* auditions, and you'll see what I mean. Many people are convinced they're gifted in ways they are not, and their so-called friends don't have the courage to correct them. It's unkind to belittle people like the "mean judge" on a TV competition, but false praise is equally destructive. Consider Romans 3:12:

> All have turned aside; together they have become worthless;
> no one does good,
> not even one.

4 Marvin R. Vincent, *Word Studies in the New Testament*, vol. 1 (Charles Scribner's Sons, 1887), 70.

"Good" here is *chrēstotēs*. Apart from God, we cannot do kindness; our works are worthless—useless.[5] Verse 13 continues to say that deceptive speech is not only useless but also deadly, likening false speech to the venom of snakes—an image that takes us back to Eden, the serpent, and the fall. Dishonest words are a severe unkindness.

Romans 3:12–13 also references several psalms that reveal what God thinks of flattery; it is unprofitable in the most extreme sense because it pleasantly paves the way to death (Pss. 5:6–10; 14:1–4). Deception is deadly and flattery is fatal. Furthermore, flattery is not only unkind but also unloving, for love "rejoices with the truth" (1 Cor. 13:6). While the truth may sting, it leads to life:

> Let a righteous man strike me—it is a kindness;
> let him rebuke me—it is oil for my head. (Ps. 141:5)

Truthfulness is also essential to friendship:

> Faithful are the wounds of a friend;
> profuse are the kisses of an enemy. (Prov. 27:6)

If we are not being truthful, we are not being useful. If we are not being useful, we are not being kind. We are not being true friends.

So what does this mean for our musical worship? Most immediately, we must take care that our lyrics don't err toward false comfort but are unafraid to confront, convict, and confess sin.

5 BDAG 1090.

More particularly, as we coordinate our ministries, we will have to navigate roles and relationships with discernment. Having a heart for worship is not enough to qualify someone for the praise band. Here's an extreme example: Letting a tone-deaf but well-meaning person sing a solo would not be useful to your congregation, which would be distracted and unable to sing along. It also would not be useful to the individual, who would be unknowingly humiliated.

All Christians are called to make melody with their hearts, but not all Christians are called to make melody with a microphone (Eph. 5:19).

In leading worship, a truthful but gracious way to show kindness to someone who lacks self-awareness is to apply the twin principles of "not this" and "not yet." "Not this" means that instead of a blanket rejection, we can guide volunteers away from an area of service where they are not qualified and work with them to find a role that is both useful to the congregation and fulfilling to the individual.

"Not yet" acknowledges volunteers' desire to serve as good and encourages them that they will be welcome to do so with appropriate preparation or maturation. I have had brilliant students who were eager to perform, but I have learned to withhold certain opportunities until I feel that they are (1) musically prepared and (2) mature enough to understand that playing for worship is about encouraging others in praise—not garnering praise for themselves.

Not all gifts or opportunities are for all people, all situations, or all seasons. Kindness calls us to exercise discernment and honesty as we guide volunteers toward satisfying service that will "excel in building up the church" (1 Cor. 14:12).

Kindness Bestows Honor

I placed honesty before honor in this chapter because Scripture repeatedly warns against speech that puffs up rather than builds up (Rom. 16:18; 1 Thess. 2:5). If we exclusively point out one another's deficiencies, however, we are also being untruthful by ignoring what is praiseworthy. A critical spirit is to honesty what flattery is to honor—a false extreme. Just as any friendship built on flattery will grow selfish and fickle, any relationship built on criticism will grow bitter and cynical. Even as we treat one another with honesty and discernment, we should not withhold honor and encouragement.

Rejoicing with the truth calls us to do just that: rejoice.

Scripture commands us to "outdo" one another in showing honor—literally, to "lead the way" in honoring others (Rom. 12:10).[6] Unlike flattery, honor is concerned with "substantial value" and "real worth."[7] As worship leaders, our job is to lead the charge in praising God, but we should also be the first to praise what is godly in others. When we lead our people in song, we should also strive to show them what biblical honor sounds like. It is a sweet, sweet sound (Prov. 16:24).

While we know that our lyrics must not shy away from tough truths, we owe it to one another to also proclaim the reality of forgiveness, freedom, life, and hope in Christ. And while our songs must praise God above all, they can also encourage Christians in specific, bold ways. This is one of many reasons I love the hymn "Thy Strong Word," which sings, "Glorious now, we

6 BDAG 869.

7 Bill Mounce, "Τιμή," Bill Mounce website, accessed February 21, 2025, https://www.billmounce.com/greek-dictionary/time.

press toward glory."[8] We should not be afraid to identify those worshiping beside us as glorious now and destined for splendor (2 Cor. 3:18; Eph. 5:27).

Many worship leaders have the opportunity to build up their congregations by speaking between songs. I often hear leaders say things like, "Wow, you're more energetic than the early service!" or "Come on, is that the loudest you can sing?" These statements are intended to promote participation, but why are we so quick to do so by comparing our congregations to others or urging them to do more? What if we encouraged engagement by *honoring* them? Worship leaders who address their congregations might consider exchanging correction for recognition and comparison for encouragement. Statements such as "I know it's early, but I'm so glad you're all here!" or "I am amazed that so many of you came to worship! Let's make the most of this time" are more positive, even as they maintain this core message: Sing like you mean it!

In rehearsals, leaders can offer more specific encouragement. Showing "honor to whom honor is owed" means not withholding praise when it is true and timely (Rom. 13:7). When a team member is doing valuable work or growing in maturity, it is right to recognize this. When our ensembles are living and singing harmoniously, we should take note. We commonly stop during rehearsals to correct errors, but how often do we stop to offer praise? Or repeat a chorus because it was so beautiful we want it to sink in? Our rehearsals should be a place not only for working out weaknesses but for noticing, enjoying, and celebrating excellence.

8 Martin H. Franzmann, "Hymn #578: Thy Strong Word," in *Lutheran Service Book* (Concordia, 2006).

We may find ourselves withholding praise from our teams or congregations because we are rightly concerned with worshiping God alone. But we worship the very "God of endurance and encouragement" (Rom. 15:5). Encouragement is part of his character. He is glorified when his people are edified, and we honor Christ when we honor his bride.

Be Kind to Yourself

Ministry workers are facing a discouragement epidemic. Those who lead their churches in praise are often left exhausted and downtrodden. Our culture tends to combat such discouragement with maxims such as "Be kind to yourself." Is there a godly way to do this? While society means that we must accept ourselves and cut ourselves slack, Christian kindness requires self-reflection and reliance on God's kindness to us.

As with kindness toward others, treating ourselves kindly requires honesty. We must invite God to "search" us and reveal areas in need of sanctification (Ps. 139:23–24). We need to take careful stock of our strengths and weaknesses. We may need to apply the principles of "not this" and "not yet" to ourselves.

We must evaluate our capabilities so we can practice effectively and lead excellently. This may mean learning music that stretches us. But it might also mean embracing practicality. I've found that what is most useful to my congregation is not necessarily virtuosity but attainability. This is good news for those who struggle to prepare new music week after week. The mark of useful worship is not the mind-boggling performances of leaders but the wholehearted participation of congregations. Don't be afraid to repeat the simpler, familiar songs that your people sing well. Don't pressure yourself to make every Sunday a novel, jaw-dropping experience unless it will build up your congregation—not just your self-esteem.

Treating ourselves with honesty also means welcoming feedback from trusted individuals such as team members, musicians in our congregations, and other staff members. I've found anonymous surveys helpful. During rehearsals, ask team members, "What did you hear?" or "What suggestions do you have?" instead of "Do you have any questions?" This fosters greater forthrightness because it assumes they have input and communicates that you want to hear it.

But what about encouragement? If you're anything like me, you're already aware of your deficiencies and would like to be cheered on now and then. We can look to the book of Numbers for refreshment. Amid strict requirements for right worship, God says to Aaron, "I give your priesthood as a gift, and any outsider who comes near shall be put to death" (Num. 18:7). The priesthood was a precious, protected privilege. God then tells Aaron that he and his sons will have no inheritance among the tribes of Israel. But if the priesthood is a gift, why are Aaron and his sons thus deprived? Because, God says, "*I* am your portion and your inheritance" (18:20). What greater portion could the priests receive? What is a parcel of land compared to an omnipotent, omnipresent God?

Let's never forget that our vocation is an honor. Like the priesthood, leading worship is a weighty responsibility—a "yoke." But it is also a unique blessing from the Lord. In his abundant kindness, God has entrusted us with the praise of his people. Even when our ministry feels like it takes more than it gives, the Lord himself is our inheritance: "Our shield and portion" forever.[9]

Music, Usefulness, and Friendship

Outside of the church, joining a musical ensemble can be an excellent way to make friends. How much more so should congregational singing help us treat one another usefully and forge genuine friendships as Christians? Musical worship is an ideal medium for cultivating true kindness because it requires tuning, invites vulnerability, and instills courage.

Tuning

It is pure bliss when a choir ends a song with a perfectly balanced chord. Such cadences are sure to send shivers of delight down my spine. But such tuning does not just happen. It requires intense focus as singers align pitch, vowel shape, and tone. Like tuning, kindness requires careful observation and evaluation. We have to invest in our volunteers, taking the time to discern their strengths and weaknesses and to ensure that they are prepared to serve to the best of their abilities.

Such kindness extends beyond just musical preparedness. Leading worship often seems to be as much about balancing needs as it is about balancing chords. While it is probably not feasible to be deeply involved in the lives of everyone in our congregations, we should be aware of the situations of those on our teams. We need to pay attention to the perfectionist who needs a comforting word, the disruptive volunteer who needs

9 John Newton, "Amazing Grace! (How Sweet the Sound)," Hymnary.org, 1779 https://hymnary.org/.

tactful correction, or the lonely man who just needs a place to sing. Before we can meet the real needs of others, we must be attuned to them.

Vulnerability

In chapter 2, I wrote about the first time I heard the "Erbarme Dich" from Bach's *St. Matthew Passion*. It cut me to the heart and still does. Music penetrates the depths of our souls, illuminating the dark crevices we would prefer to keep hidden. If we let it, music can convict us deeply, even painfully. While I've been intellectually moved by sermons, I have been most powerfully and painfully moved by music. And while I may take notes during an excellent message, a rousing hymn can bring tears to my eyes. Music invites a level of openness that is essential for a change of heart. The right song can crack us open and force us to reckon with what pours out without feeling browbeaten.

When I am wrestling with something, my brokenness often pours out in song more readily than speech. Similarly, people tend to be more comfortable expressing vulnerability in corporate singing than in day-to-day conversation. Musical worship creates a much-needed space to be honest with God, ourselves, and those beside us. It invites us to face our weaknesses and remember our dependence on our kind Savior.

Courage

I have an odd but effective antidote to anxiety: bagpipe music on full blast. Something about the astringent timbre of bagpipes invigorates my vaguely Scottish blood and prepares me for battle—or a busy workday. As anyone who has jogged on a treadmill without earbuds can attest, few things are as motivating as music. It gives us strength. There's a reason the soundtrack of human history includes so many work and war songs—and worship songs can be both at once.

While we want to avoid emotional manipulation, our music should be motivating. Even as we allow space for honesty and vulnerability, we should want to send our people away encouraged—literally filled with courage. As worship leaders, we get to choose our people's fight songs. We should include music that gets them fired up to "run with endurance the race that is set before us" (Heb. 12:1).

Closing Hymn: "What a Friend We Have in Jesus"

Joseph Medlicott Scriven (1819–1886) was well aware of his need for divine friendship. His poor health forced him to give up a military career. Twice, he was about to be married only for his fiancée to die unexpectedly. He labored tirelessly to serve the poor and disabled as a teacher. Understandably, he battled depression throughout his life.[10]

Though this hymn is widely known today, Scriven originally wrote it to encourage his mother through a difficult season. Its composition was an act of familial kindness. Scriven then kept it as a personal anthem to sing in the face of discouragement—to lighten sorrow's load by pointing him back to Christ, whose yoke is kind and friendship unwavering. Like Scriven, let's use our songs to build others up through conviction and comfort, honesty and honor, truth and grace.

10 Bert Polman, "Joseph Medlicott Scriven," Hymnary.org, accessed March 12, 2024, https://hymnary.org/.

What a friend we have in Jesus,
All our sins and griefs to bear!
What a privilege to carry
Everything to God in prayer!
O what peace we often forfeit,
O what needless pain we bear,
All because we do not carry
Everything to God in prayer!

Have we trials and temptations?
Is there trouble anywhere?
We should never be discouraged;
Take it to the Lord in prayer!
Can we find a friend so faithful
Who will all our sorrows share?
Jesus knows our every weakness;
Take it to the Lord in prayer!

Are we weak and heavy laden,
Cumbered with a load of care?
Precious Savior, still our refuge—
Take it to the Lord in prayer!
Do your friends despise, forsake you?
Take it to the Lord in prayer!
In his arms he'll take and shield you;
You will find a solace there.[11]

11 Joseph Medlicott Scriven, "What a Friend We Have in Jesus," Hymnary.org, 1855, https://hymnary.org/.

Discussion/Reflection

1. Do you agree that kindness is costly? Has true kindness ever cost you anything?

2. Reflect on a time someone shared a tough truth with you. Did you consider this kindness?

3. Do you ever find yourself withholding praise from others? Resolve to encourage your team or congregation in three specific ways this week.

4. Do you view your ministry as an honor from the Lord? Take time to thank God for his kindness to you.

5. What type of music bolsters your courage? What songs seem to fill your congregation with courage? Program a few of these in the upcoming weeks.

6

Goodness

Our Musical Offering

For we are his workmanship, created in Christ Jesus for good works, which God prepared beforehand, that we should walk in them.

EPHESIANS 2:10

I HAVE ALWAYS STRUGGLED with stage fright. When preparing for my capstone recital as a piano major, I was panicky beyond reason. Trembling backstage, I envied the composure of other musicians, who performed with ease and relished the spotlight. (To this day, I have nightmares in which I must play a high-stakes recital without practicing.) Wallowing in fearful self-consciousness (another side of pride), I transposed the precious gifts of my skill and education into a self-made curse.

At last, a mentor told me that to overcome my nerves I needed to regain my appreciation of music as a gift, and to do so, I needed to focus on giving. So I played for my parents, who nurtured my passion from a young age; my teachers, who challenged and prayed for me; my peers, who refined me; and my friends, who bore with me through my stress. My worry diminished sharply when I stopped focusing on what I lacked—natural confidence on stage—but on what I could give.

My recital was not perfect, but it was a present.

Perhaps you've been told "Music is a gift from God" so many times that it sounds trite. This doesn't make it any less true, though. Music is a gift. Moreover, it's a gift that is meant to be returned—offered back to God as we pour into his people (Prov. 19:17; Matt. 25:40). Even when stewing in performance anxiety, I played decently. And yet, my music lacked true goodness, which calls us to enjoy and share God's generosity. Especially in musical worship, we are commissioned to play and sing *for* others, not just *before* them.

The Fulfilling Fruit

In worship, music and offerings are often inextricable. We may have soloists sing while passing the offering plate or feature times of "musical offerings" apart from monetary giving. For years, I wondered, If music is our offering to God, shouldn't everyone be singing? But just as tithing supports church operations, our music is a gift to the Lord because it is also a gift *to the church*. We offer our music—like our finances—to God as we use it to build up his people. Goodness invites us to reframe every aspect of musical worship as an offering: an opportunity to enjoy and use the gifts of God to do good to "those who are of the household of faith" (Gal. 6:10).

Just as we use *good* in English to mean delicious, pleasant, acceptable, polite, reliable, and beautiful, *good* and *goodness* are used broadly throughout Scripture to refer to charitable deeds, useful things, well-made items, and upright people. As a fruit of the Spirit, "goodness" (*agathōsunē*) involves all of these concepts but essentially boils down to generosity. More specifically, it is God's generosity working through us to promote the welfare of others.[1] Spiritual fruits such as goodness testify to God's generosity as he fills us with his Spirit and enables us to produce godly fruit where we formerly practiced fleshly works. Whereas the works of the flesh led us to hoard things for ourselves, the fruit of the Spirit builds up the body of Christ as God shares his character with us and calls us to treat others with the same generosity—to fill them as we have been filled.

In addition to the fruit of the Spirit, God gives individuals specific gifts for the building up of the church (Rom. 12:3–8; 1 Cor. 12:1–31). These fruits and gifts are not meant to be enjoyed in isolation. God's generosity is not meant to be contained but to overflow. Just as an overfull cup cannot help spilling onto the surfaces around it, God's overwhelming goodness toward us compels us to live and sing generously toward others.

Agathōsunē appears only a few times in the New Testament, Greek translations of the Old Testament, and in writings about or dependent on Scripture. It is in this sense a uniquely

1 Frederick William Danker, ed., *A Greek-English Lexicon of the New Testament and Other Early Christian Literature*, 3rd ed. (University of Chicago Press, 2000), 2–4; hereafter BDAG.

Christian word. R. C. Trench cites *agathōsunē* as an example of how "revealed religion has enriched the later language of Greece."[2] This observation offers insight into the nature of goodness as a fruit of the Spirit; it enriches everything it touches, from languages to lives.

Envy's Enemy

The fruit of the Spirit is listed in opposition to the works of the flesh, and goodness is the archenemy of envy (Gal. 5:21). In stark contrast to lifegiving, satiating generosity, envy is rotten and unsatisfying. It consumes its victims from the inside out, spoiling and withering everything it touches.[3] It causes us to obsess over what we do not have as we seek our own gain. Goodness expels envy as it guides us to use what we do have to benefit others. Ironically and wonderfully, self-giving goodness leads to fulfillment, whereas self-serving envy leads only to a vicious cycle of anxiety and emptiness.

In theological terms, envy renders us *incurvatus in se*: "curved in" on ourselves. Author and worship leader Zac Hicks describes "curved in" worship as worship that makes us think more and more about ourselves—how we are feeling, doing, appearing, and so on.[4] Such "curved in" worship is more likely to breed envy than to generate goodness as it tempts us to look inward rather than upward and outward.

2 R. C. Trench, *Trench's Synonyms of the New Testament*, ed. Robert G. Hoerber, et al. (Baker, 1989), 247.

3 BDAG 1054–55.

4 Zac Hicks, "What Worship Curved in on Itself Looks Like," *Zac Hicks* (blog), November 19, 2013, https://zachicks.com/.

If, like me, you struggle with envy and anxiety, you may be looking in the wrong direction. Great musicians overcome their fear by focusing on sharing their music—reveling in its beauty and presenting it to their audiences as a gift. They cannot waste time and energy worrying over the pieces they have not learned or the nuances they have yet to master. For their time on stage, their best bet is to set aside self-consciousness in favor of self-giving. Only by looking beyond ourselves can we play and sing with openness and enjoyment.

Whether we serve smaller churches in rural areas or megachurches with massive platforms, the questions we must answer are the same: Will we give what we have or grieve what we don't? Will we waste away with envy or pour ourselves out in generosity? Will we be jealous of others or zealous to use whatever gifts God has seen fit to give us to his glory?

Filled with All Knowledge

Among the authors of Scripture, Paul alone uses *agathōsunē* for goodness. Theologian Marvin R. Vincent suggests that this is to identify this type of goodness as a "zeal for truth which rebukes, corrects, and chastises, as Christ when he purged the temple."[5] This certainly seems to be the case when Paul praises the Roman believers for being "full of goodness, filled with all knowledge and able to instruct one another" (Rom. 15:14). These Christians are ravenous for the word, eager to understand their faith and teach it to others correctly.

To be full of goodness, we must be continually filling ourselves with knowledge of the truth. Goodness is not just about getting our

5 Marvin R. Vincent, *Word Studies in the New Testament*, vol. 3 (Charles Scribner's Sons, 1887), 35.

doctrine basically right; it loves the truth ardently. Good worship songs should be saturated with Scripture. Like a hearty meal, our singing should satiate people with the meat of God's word.

Sometimes I think we phone it in when it comes to our lyrics. So long as they are not *un*true, we let them slide and, well, put them on the slides. But is this fulfilling in the long run? If goodness is generosity, shouldn't we give our people lyrics that will fill them up? Scripture invites us to use singing to teach the word with "*all* wisdom" and let it dwell in us "richly" (Col. 3:16).

Not just acceptably—*richly.*

Like the women who send me home with containers full of leftovers after church potlucks, we should be hospitably determined to provide solid lyrics for our people to chew on and digest throughout the week.

I'm not suggesting that every song needs to be a systematic theology. Some of the most powerful, truthful songs I know are relatively simple. As with gift-giving, simplicity is not the problem; stinginess is. Indeed, simplicity may at times be more generous, for it allows more worshipers to sing with understanding and renders lyrics easier to remember throughout the week. In any case, whether the words we sing are simple or complex, they must communicate the riches of God's word.

When we sing truth-filled lyrics, we aren't just showing off our knowledge or memorizing Scripture arbitrarily. It is not a theoretical exercise, but a way of preparing us to apply our theology in our lives. It's a way of internalizing the word so that we can draw on its wisdom and comfort in our darkest hours. Before she passed away, my husband's grandmother suffered extreme dementia. And yet, she remembered her favorite hymns. Their melodies kept God's promises hidden in her heart when her mind faltered. Through memorable music, good worship songs work their truths into the deepest recesses of ourselves. Like hearty protein, they provide sustenance throughout our lives and to the moment of our deaths.

Worship leader, give your people what they need most: a way to reflect on God's word now and to recall it in their darkest hours.

Filled with Resolve

"I have stored up your word in my heart that I might not sin against you" (Ps. 119:11). By helping us store Scripture in our hearts, musical worship offers a safeguard against sin. It's difficult to speak ungraciously when I have the gospel playing in my head to the tune of "Amazing Grace." It's harder to be selfish when "Jesus Paid It All" is looping through my brain. It's pretty tough to lash out in anger when "It Is Well with My Soul" is echoing between my ears.

Another definition of *agathōsunē* is "uprightness of heart and life."[6] When we sing together, we equip and motivate one another to pursue this good life. As worship leaders, we give our people songs as weapons against sin and discouragement. As participants, we lend one another courage and strength as our voices join in celebrating God's goodness and committing to obedience. It's no coincidence that Ephesians 5, which calls Christians to cultivate "all that is good and right and true" (5:9) culminates in a call to song (5:1–20).

6 Joseph H. Thayer, *Thayer's Greek-English Lexicon of the New Testament* (1889; repr., Hendrickson, 2023), 3.

When studying abroad in England, I was warned to stay in my flat during a high-stakes football match. Local fans seemed ready for war as they marched through town, singing their teams' songs. I'm not sure who they were trying to motivate—the players on TV or their fellow fans—but they sure were zealous. Singing together should likewise stoke our zeal as Christians. Even apart from lyrics our music can strengthen our resolve and motivate action. There's a reason I don't usually end services with slow, somber pieces. I want to give people an energy boost as they start their week, courtesy of a final hymn with a martial beat or an exhilarating postlude. While peace and patience lead us to protect moments of stillness and introspection, goodness reminds us that we should not be afraid to use music "to stir up one another to love and good works" (Heb. 10:24).

At the same time, the zeal of *agathōsunē* is not merely an emotional drive. It is an earnestness that presses us to act. Our songs should not just rile up our emotions but direct us toward specific, God-honoring disciplines. Remember, Paul links being full of goodness with being "filled with all knowledge and able to instruct one another" (Rom. 15:14). Our singing should not only be informative and inspiring but *instructive*.

Have you ever received an intricate gift that didn't come with an instruction manual? Don't do that to your congregations. Be sure that your songs also tell them how to apply the truth and channel their zeal. This is why I love hymns such as "Rise! To Arms! With Prayer, Employ You," which is laden with imperatives: Rise! Pray! Wield the word! Cast off sin! Be steadfast! Trust the Lord! Run![7]

7 Wilhelm Erasmus Arends, "Rise! To Arms! With Prayer Employ You," trans. John M. Sloan, Hymnary.org, 1714, https://hymnary.org/.

This song is a war cry, at once rallying the troops and offering battle plans against sin.

In all this, it helps to pray that God would use our music to "fulfill every resolve for good and every work of faith by his power, so that the name of our Lord Jesus may be glorified" (2 Thess. 1:11–12).

Filled with All Craftsmanship

Because the type of goodness listed among the fruit of the Spirit focuses heavily on truthfulness and uprightness, you might wonder whether it includes any sense of artistry.[8] Trying to imagine "good" worship apart from beautiful music is difficult.

But take heart: Goodness is rooted in God's generosity.

So is music. So is beauty.

We don't need music to survive. And yet, God not only allows but commands singing. The fact that Scripture repeatedly tells us to sing is a testament to God's generosity; he requires us to worship in a way that is truthful, obedient, and *enjoyable*. Singing is not merely a vehicle for knowledge and zeal; it's a genuinely fulfilling activity. We should not be afraid to enjoy stunning music—the type of music that leaves us thinking, "Now, *that* was good!"

Throughout Scripture, the Holy Spirit is active not only in empowering moral goodness but in equipping artistry. We are told in no uncertain terms to be filled with the Spirit and to sing—not just to sermonize and serve (Eph. 5:19). In *Art for God's Sake*, Philip Ryken points out that the first man

8 Another word often translated as "good" (*kalos*) refers to beauty as well, particularly the beauty of wisdom and virtue.

Scripture identifies as being filled with the Spirit is an artist.[9] When giving instructions for constructing the tabernacle, God tells Moses:

> I have called by name Bezalel . . . and I have filled him with the Spirit of God, with ability and intelligence, with knowledge and all craftsmanship, to devise artistic designs, to work in gold, silver, and bronze, in cutting stones for setting, and in carving wood, to work in every craft. And behold, I have appointed with him Oholiab. . . . And I have given to all able men ability, that they may make all that I have commanded you. (Ex. 31:2-6)

The surrounding chapters record God's stipulations for proper worship. Here, he selects men to beautify his place of worship. Moreover, he sends his very Spirit to ensure that they are fully equipped for the task. Isn't this marvelous? The Spirit of truth, who produces the fruit of goodness, also imbues these chosen artists with "all craftsmanship" (Ex. 31:3).

God cares intimately about artistry. Beauty matters.

The point of this chapter is not to descend into debates about aesthetics. Instead, I simply urge you not to make artistic decisions arbitrarily. Remember that God gave Bezalel intelligence as well as skill. Think carefully about your musical and technical decisions, from the songs you introduce to the styles you include. Seriously weigh your choices to discern what will best suit your ensemble and congregation.

9 Philip Graham Ryken, *Art for God's Sake: A Call to Recover the Arts* (P&R, 2006), 21–22.

Keep refining your skills so, like Bezalel, you are ready to perform the tasks God calls you to with excellence. Keep honing and expanding your abilities. Try arranging, songwriting, or composition. Listen to other artists and attend different services. Experiment with elements from other genres when appropriate. Dig into the details. Play with nuances of phrasing, articulation, and instrumentation. Treasure the best of tradition. Be open to innovation. Don't be afraid to explore and enjoy the artistry of worship; making beautiful music is a way of reveling in and reflecting God's generosity.

Give Good Gifts

When my mom gives gifts, she wraps them with care. In this way, an everyday item like a frying pan becomes a gift rather than just a useful item. Meanwhile, my husband gives gifts in whatever packaging they arrive in. The contents are solid, but the presentation is lacking. Still, this is better than my cat's approach. To her, content doesn't matter, but an empty box is bliss.

Because our music is a gift, we should care about content and presentation. *What* we sing (the content of our songs) is paramount, but the "wrapping" does matter. If it didn't, we could worship by repeating facts in a monotone. Instead, our God invites us to sing, an activity that presumes not just knowledge and obedience but creativity.

Leaders, let's be thoughtful givers. Let's choose songs that will fill our people with truth and resolve as well as satisfy their God-given yearning for beauty.

Participants and volunteers, you are also called to generous singing. Nothing is more encouraging to worship leaders than a singing church. Enthusiastic participation is your gift to them and to those around you, who will sing more freely when you do. Don't be self-conscious or envious. Share your voice—be it strong or soft, trained or trying its best—with your leaders and neighbors.

Reframing Our Roles

As worship leaders, we have to wear many hats (maybe literally). Considering your role through the following lenses may help you identify areas relevant to goodness that need refinement. But this exercise is also meant to affirm your good work as you balance multiple responsibilities.

That said, if you are a worship leader, you are also a collaborator, coach, creator, curator, and God's craftsmanship.

A Collaborator

As a collaborative pianist, I don't usually call the shots, but I help them hit home. It's my job to lend support to soloists as I (in the words of a nonmusical friend) "make singing less awkward."

Similarly, it's our responsibility as worship leaders to work alongside our pastors, using music to accompany and reinforce their teaching. When my husband preached on Isaiah 53, he provided a wealth of historical context, exegetical information, and practical application. Our worship team then worked the passion of that passage into our bones with songs such as "Man of Sorrows" and "What Wondrous Love Is This?" Just as a capable accompanist is a gift to his or her soloists, an intentional worship leader is a gift to his or her pastor.

A Coach

When I play the hymn "Fight the Good Fight," I use a baseball organ riff as an introduction.[10] I like watching my choir members mouth "Charge!" before they begin singing. The verses that inspired this hymn include athletic imagery to drive home their point, so why shouldn't I use athletic sound effects to establish a sense of determination? (1 Tim. 6:12). Worship leaders are like coaches. We set the tone and energy for our services. Like a coach giving a pep talk, we can use music to get our people fired up.

If there's one thing I've learned from my sports-loving husband, it's that a tough coach is a gift to dedicated players. Through biblical and instructive lyrics, we also push our people to recite the "playbook" (Scripture) and run the "plays" (spiritual disciplines). Our worship services are a place to practice our defense and to strengthen our people for the challenges ahead.

A Creator

It's easy to get bogged down by the demand of weekly services and rehearsals. While I love music ministry, it sometimes feels like it inhibits my "real" creative work. But this is untrue. Worship leading involves constant creativity. We have to figure out how to make songs recorded by professionals suit our volunteers. We may have to revise lyrics to be more singable or biblical. We may not be composing symphonies, but we have to arrange transitions, introductions, and instrumentals.

10 See John S. B. Monsell, "Fight the Good Fight," Hymnary.org, 1863, https://hymnary.org/.

Let's not devalue our creativity just because it doesn't look like a movie montage of a famous composer. We are called to be creative in an urgent, practical, ever-fluctuating way as we prepare music for our unique contexts and congregations.

A Curator

As worship leaders, we have the privilege of deciding what music to share with our congregations. It's our job to seek, discover, and polish up gems—songs that deserve to be heard and sung. This is one of the most exciting aspects of our work. I love passing out a new piece of music to my choir, knowing it may soon become one of their favorite songs.

Just as gallery curators excel because they immerse themselves in visual art, our worship will be enhanced when we allow ourselves space to simply enjoy music. We may feel we are always putting out music but never taking it in. I've found, though, that I play best on Sundays when I make time during the week to play music for fun—even if those pieces never make it into a service. As we curate services for our congregations, let's not forget that God gives us music for our refreshment as well.

God's Craftsmanship

As we work to make good music, let's not forget that *we* are God's "workmanship, created in Christ Jesus for good works, which God prepared beforehand, that we should walk in them" (Eph. 2:10). Music is an instrument that God uses to form us. When we gather to sing, it's not just about what we are doing but what God is doing to, in, and through us. The goal of our worship, then, is not merely to perform good music but to be prepared for good works that testify to God's generosity.

Closing Hymn: "Come Thou Fount"

I cannot think of a better hymn to conclude this chapter than "Come Thou Fount." Praise for God's generosity, gospel truth, obedient action, and melodious singing—this hymn has it all. It reminds us that "every good gift and every perfect gift is from above, coming down from the Father of lights, with whom there is no variation or shadow due to change" (James 1:17). Our musical gifts should point us toward God the highest giver and Christ the truest gift.

The line "tune my heart" is especially wonderful, leading me to imagine God as a master luthier, adjusting our heartstrings with care and skill. This line also captures the reality that, in worship, *we* are the primary instruments. Like Bezalel, we will do our best work when we offer ourselves to God and let him work through us.

Come, thou Fount of every blessing;
Tune my heart to sing thy grace;
Streams of mercy, never ceasing,
Call for songs of loudest praise.
Teach me some melodious sonnet,
Sung by flaming tongues above;
Praise the mount! I'm fixed upon it,
Mount of God's unchanging love!

Here I raise my Ebenezer;
Hither by thy help I'm come;
And I hope, by thy good pleasure,

Safely to arrive at home.
Jesus sought me when a stranger;
Wand'ring from the fold of God:
He, to rescue me from danger,
Interposed his precious blood.

O to grace how great a debtor
Daily I'm constrained to be!
Let thy goodness, like a fetter,
Bind my wand'ring heart to thee.
Prone to wander, Lord, I feel it,
Prone to leave the God I love;
Here's my heart; O take and seal it;
Seal it for thy courts above.[11]

Reflection/Discussion

1. Have you ever thought about music as a gift to your listeners as well as to God? Is there a specific song you'd like to share with your congregation in the coming weeks?

2. Are you struggling with envy? List the abilities and resources God has given you and think creatively about how you can use these to fill others.

3. Pick a song from your most recent service and try to match a Scripture reference to each line. Based on this exercise, is this song filling your people with truth?

11 Robert Robinson, "Come, Thou Fount of Every Blessing," Hymnary.org, 1758, https://hymnary.org/.

4. Which of the five roles of worship leaders stood out to you the most: collaborator, coach, creator, curator, or God's craftsmanship? Why?

5. Name a song that made you think, "Wow, that is good!" the first time you heard it. What about it struck you so powerfully?

7

Faithfulness

Playing Note by Note

One who is faithful in a very little is also faithful in much, and one who is dishonest in a very little is also dishonest in much.

LUKE 16:10

THE MUSIC STAND would not, well, stand. I had to prop two hymnals under it to make it sturdy enough to support my sheet music. Once it was stable, I took in my surroundings: a church basement, the walls lined with portraits of previous pastors. This silent crowd easily outnumbered the congregants sitting before me, fiddling with folding chairs and distracted by the smell of baked potatoes wafting in from the kitchen.

I led the music and sat through the message. My watch hinted that if I rushed through the offertory and left immediately after the final hymn, I could hit the grocery store before teaching lessons all afternoon. I could skip several pages of my solo and cut the postlude entirely, and nobody would be any the wiser.

But I didn't. I played on—not because I'm all that great, but because I was convicted by the bridge from one of my own songs:

> If I can't be faithful
> With the broken and little,
> How can I be trusted with more?[1]

Giving our all onstage—where we receive applause and accumulate followings—is a human accomplishment. Worshiping week after week in anonymity, with broken instruments, in unglamorous settings, or before small congregations—well, that's a spiritual feat.

That's faithfulness.

The Functional Fruit

The word translated as "faithfulness" in Galatians 5:22 is *pistis*, which primarily means belief. As a fruit of the Spirit, *pistis* refers to "that which evokes trust and faith" or, more to the point, "the state of being someone in whom confidence can be placed."[2] Faithfulness demands reliability and trustworthiness. Faithful people do what they say they will do. For Christians, this dependability is rooted in our dependence on God. Our faithfulness is the outworking of our faith.

1 Ryanne Molinari, "The Season of Broken Things," *Ryanne Molinari* (blog), March 13, 2025, https://ryannemolinari.com/.

2 Frederick William Danker, ed., *A Greek-English Lexicon of the New Testament and Other Early Christian Literature*, 3rd ed. (University of Chicago Press, 2000), 818.

If I had a microphone that failed to make my voice louder, I'd deem it nonfunctional. Its name advertises its intended function: to amplify sound. As people of faith, our function is faithfulness. We must believe *and* bear fruit; our faith must yield faithfulness (John 15:8). The phrase "trustworthy Christians" ought to be redundant. Faithfulness should just be who we are, one of our most basic qualities as people saved by grace through faith.

Faithfulness is belief in action. We believe God is steadfast, so we serve steadily. We believe he keeps his promises, so we are consistent in word and deed. We believe God provides according to his wisdom, so we steward our resources. We believe God established days and seasons, so we labor and rest appropriately. We believe God alone is sovereign, so we do our best and leave the results in his hands.

Proverbs 3:5–6 is clearly about faith. But these familiar verses are also about faithfulness:

> Trust in the LORD with all your heart,
> and do not lean on your own understanding.
> In all your ways acknowledge him,
> and he will make straight your paths.

If we really trust the Lord to direct our paths, we will walk them—step by step—in confidence.

Steadfast Love

The unhinged, up-and-down artist is a stereotype for a reason. As a creative activity, music-making demands some degree of spontaneity and expression. But we are people of faith before we are people of song. Whatever our eccentricities, we must be characterized by stability.

When initially studying faithfulness, I noticed two crucial details. First, Scripture overwhelmingly focuses on God's faithfulness. Ours depends completely on his. Second, God's faithfulness is overwhelmingly coupled with his "steadfast love."[3] Faithfulness is inextricable from steadfastness—from unwavering integrity. And yet, steadfastness is not bland and apathetic. It isn't just going through the motions like a musical automaton—reliable but heartless. Steadfastness is *loving*. For example, I know a pastor who once cross-country skied to church. In the dead of winter, there was no other way to get there. I imagine that the few congregants who managed to attend that week felt loved by his extreme reliability.

Leaders, when our pastors, teams, and congregations can rely on us to show up and do our best no matter what, we are acting not only faithfully but lovingly. Laypeople, you have the opportunity to love your leaders and fellow worshipers by regularly gathering to sing—come wind, rain, snow, or sleet, or anxiety, fatigue, joy, or grief. Through steadfastness, we point one another to the Lord, whose faithful love sustains us. Steadfast participation—as much as sudden praise—is worship.

Steady Wins the Race

We all know the moral "Slow and steady wins the race." I'm not sure about slow—we are told to *run* the race of faith—but steadiness is definitely the winning strategy (1 Cor. 9:24; Heb. 12:1). Those

3 Of the forty-six times that God's faithfulness is directly mentioned, thirty also reference his steadfast love.

who work steadily and honestly will reap abundance, but those who exchange faithfulness for speedy gain will suffer in the end:

> A faithful man will abound with blessings,
> but whoever hastens to be rich will not go unpunished.
> (Prov. 28:20)

In our age of immediacy and self-promotion, individuals seeking greater influence can buy followers from individuals seeking greater income. But faithfulness has no shortcuts. It cannot be forged all at once in sudden success. Instead, it is cultivated over the course of a lifetime through one God-honoring decision after another.

John Newton, the writer of "Amazing Grace," offers this advice to Christians seeking to live a faithful life: "A Christian is not of hasty growth, like a mushroom, but rather like the oak, the progress of which is hardly perceptible but in time becomes a deep-rooted tree."[4] Did you know that oaks are among the most wind-resistant trees? They don't grow rapidly, but they do grow resilient.

When we stand before the Lord, our lives will be measured not by how many of our songs went viral or how many standing ovations we received but by steadfast faithfulness. This may not seem like much right now, but like the imperceptible growth of giant trees, if we hold steady, we will prove spiritually immense and immovable (2 Tim. 4:8).

"All My Work Be Praise"

Faithfulness is also about integrity—wholeness of character. Although we may be more outgoing or expressive while leading

4 John Newton, *Letters of John Newton: With Biographical Sketches and Notes by Josiah Bull* (Banner of Truth, 2007), 285.

worship, there should be no moral divide between who we are on Sundays and who we are throughout the week. Worship leadership does not end when we switch off our speakers. Our lives—even more than our lyrics—proclaim who we worship. In this sense, all Christians are tasked with leading worship as we make known our faithful God through faithful living.

After instructing the Colossians to sing, Paul writes, "And whatever you do, in word or deed, do everything in the name of the Lord Jesus, giving thanks to God the Father through him" (Col. 3:17). We pray and praise publicly "in Jesus's name," but what about in our private, mundane moments and tasks? Faithfulness calls us *to do everything* in the name of the Lord Jesus. Do we sort through playlists, plan our arrangements, and schedule volunteers in his name? Do we treat our families as we would our congregants, caring for them in Jesus's name? If, like me, you are a multivocational worship leader, do you manage your other jobs with the same diligence as your church work, doing even secular gigs in Jesus's name?

Whether weekday work or Sunday worship, do it all in the name of Jesus. Consider this stanza from "My Shepherd Will Supply My Need," by the prolific hymn writer Isaac Watts:

> The sure provisions of my God
> Attend me all my days.
> O may thy house be my abode,
> And all my work be praise![5]

5 Isaac Watts, "My Shepherd Will Supply My Need," Hymnary.org, 1786, https://hymnary.org/.

This is the heart of faithfulness: that everything we do would become praise as we pursue consistency in word and deed—in our worship music and in our mundane work.

Faithful in Little

I grew up in a town that seemed to have a megachurch on every corner. Imagine my surprise when I read that the majority of churches in America average sixty worshipers per Sunday.[6] This means that most of us aren't standing before enormous crowds every Sunday. And yet, whatever our church's size, we are expected to be faithful in the same proportion: 100 percent.

In the parable of the talents, a man gives money to three servants: "To one, he gave five talents, to another two, to another one, to each according to his ability" (Matt. 25:15). The five-talent servant makes a smart trade, earning five more talents: a 100 percent increase. The two-talent servant makes two more talents: also a 100 percent increase (25:20, 22). Both generate the same return on investment.

These servants have differing abilities. Accordingly, one is trusted with more money and the other with less. Both, however, make the most of the abilities and talents they have been given and are praised with the same words: "Well done, good and faithful servant. You have been faithful over a little; I will set you over much. Enter into the joy of your master" (Matt. 25:21, 23).

This parable is comforting. I don't know about you, but I had only a little say in where I ended up working. God opened those doors even as he closed other ones. And, if you're like me, you have probably

6 Christopher Watson, "Worship in the Average Church in America," *Worship Leader*, June 26, 2023, https://worshipleader.com/.

wished for more natural ability at some point or another. But God, who knows each of us best, gave us what we have and put us where we are on purpose. When we accept this, we can make the most of our situations. We don't preach a prosperity gospel that says the more faith you have, the more success you'll get. We practice faithfulness, serving resourcefully even (and perhaps especially) in littleness.

The parable of the talents is a nice motivational tale until the third servant arrives. He does not lose the talent entrusted to him, but he also does not multiply it. He buries it to keep it safe and sound (and stagnant) and comes armed with excuses.

Faithfulness is not fatalism. Contentment is not complacency. Accepting what God gives us—whether a little or a lot—means making the most of it. For instance, faithfulness means that I accept my small choir with gratitude *and* push its members to their full potential.

It's up to God to bless our investments, but woe to us if we sit on our hands and say, "God only gave me a little, so I guess that's all I have to bother with." In the parable of the talents, the master responds to the third servant with disappointment *and* righteous ire: "You wicked and slothful servant!" (Matt. 25:26). In another parable, Jesus says, "One who is faithful in a very little is also faithful in much, and one who is dishonest in a very little is also dishonest in much" (Luke 16:10). The opposite of faithfulness is not just laziness but dishonesty. It is squandering what God gave us to steward.

Especially in smaller ministries, it can become easy to mistake littleness for faithfulness, as though rejecting promotions, additional resources, further training, or even newcomers is somehow virtuous. While it is true that God often uses what is small (mustard seeds, for instance), he also tells us to be fruitful and multiply—to make disciples and grow in our faith. It is wrong to seek advancement or increase at all costs, but it is also wrong to cling to smallness—to hoard rather than to invest in the people, resources, communities, and talents God entrusts to us.

Faithful in Limits

Does your life ever feel like an endless procession of Sundays—like you barely catch your breath on Monday before having to prepare for worship all over again? Sometimes, I'll see a plaque celebrating the decades-long ministry of a previous church musician and wonder, How on earth did she do that?

The answer is like that of the old riddle: "How do you eat an elephant? One bite at a time."

How do you lead worship faithfully? One Sunday at a time.

"And which of you by being anxious can add a single hour to his span of life?" asks Jesus. "Therefore do not be anxious about tomorrow, for tomorrow will be anxious for itself. Sufficient for the day is its own trouble" (Matt. 6:27, 34). Which of us can cram a lifetime of ministry into one rehearsal? Or decades of singing into one service? Rather, as Bonhoeffer explains, "A day at a time is long enough to sustain one's faith; the next day will have its own cares."[7] We are not made to have unlimited time—not yet anyway. We are created to take life week by week, day by day.

Ephesians exhorts us to make the best use of our time and suggests singing together as one way to do so (Eph. 5:15–20). Throwing ourselves wholeheartedly into worship is faithfulness. But managing our time also means knowing when to rest. Faithfulness encourages us to expand *and accept* our limitations—to work hard

7 Dietrich Bonhoeffer, *Life Together: The Classic Exploration of Christian Community*, trans. John W. Doberstein (HarperOne, 1954), 73.

without forgetting that only God is all-powerful. He established limits for us even before the fall, ordaining patterns of labor and leisure for our benefit (Gen. 2:3; Eccl. 3:1). God didn't make us omnipresent, omniscient, omnipotent, or any other "omni" word. We cannot be everything to everyone, everywhere, all at once. While faithfulness does not allow complacency, it also keeps us from being controlling and, instead, invites us to rest confidently.

Faithfulness motivates us to practice diligently and to know when to trust our preparation. It leads us to coach other musicians but to avoid micromanaging, to call our congregations to song as well as to step back and trust them with an *a cappella* chorus. It means enduring busy seasons with excellence (I'm looking at you, Advent and Lent) and not being afraid to enjoy lighter months. Constant work might make us reliable humans, but it does not render us faithful Christians. Rest reminds us that we are not God and that we are faithful not because we are holding everything together, but because we know the one who is (Col. 1:16–17).

Faithfulness means living within God-ordained limits, trusting that he is always awake, always present, always in the know, and always in control. Believing this, we can savor both work and rest. We can take our vocations one service, one Sunday, and one season at a time, trusting that God sees the big picture and will provide for us "morning by morning."[8]

Faithfulness and Musicianship

Nothing has taught me more about faithfulness than serving in music ministry week after week. I hope that the following

8 Thomas O. Chrisholm, "Great Is Thy Faithfulness," Hymnary.org, 1923, https://hymnary.org/.

similarities between faithfulness and musicianship will deepen your understanding of and appreciation for both.

Faithfulness and Musicianship Are Accomplished Step by Step, Note by Note

I recently played for a funeral and wedding on the same day. By the end of the wedding, I was exhausted. As I looked at the final pages of music before me, my heart began to race. But the refrain from a poem famously quoted by Elisabeth Elliot came to mind: "Do the next thing."[9]

When all is said and done, that is faithfulness: doing the next thing and leaving the results to God. We cannot fit the faithfulness of a lifetime into a moment. That's a recipe for anxiety. Instead, a lifetime of faithfulness is built moment by moment.

Maybe the stack of music before you seems insurmountable. Pick the next piece. Play the next note. Maybe you're feeling so run-down that you wonder how you'll get through worship this week. Sing the next word. Play the next chord.

Taking worship "note by note" increases our resilience. The worst thing a performer can do after hitting a wrong note is stop altogether. The best approach is to keep calm and move on to the next one. Leaders, not every service will be a musical triumph. Plan the next one anyway. Laypeople, not every Sunday is going to leave you elated. Come back anyway.

How is a symphony composed? Note by note. How is faithfulness practiced? Step by step. Do the next thing.

9 Justin Taylor, "Do the Next Thing," The Gospel Coalition, October 25, 2017, https://www.thegospelcoalition.org/.

Faithfulness and Musicianship Are Developed via Imitation

When I was first learning music theory, my teacher had me copy out scores by established composers. This forced me to examine their work more closely and taught me the concepts I would need for my own. Now I teach technique and expression by having students copy my movements or phrasing. Imitation is crucial to almost every aspect of a music education.

Paul instructs us to cultivate faithfulness in much the same way, following his example as he follows Christ (1 Cor. 4:16–17). Likewise, Hebrews urges Christians to consider and imitate the faith of their leaders, teachers, and all those who came before them (Heb. 11:1–12:2).

In a culture that chases the trends and novelty of youth, we must be careful to value seasoned worship leaders. We need them as mentors and role models. Regardless of your age or experience, it helps to keep a mental list of mature leaders whose character and artistry you admire. Don't plagiarize their creative work but unashamedly imitate faithfulness wherever you find it. I frequently imagine what my mentors would do in my place, and this never fails to bolster my confidence and hone my discernment.

Faithfulness and Musicianship Demand Dependence

Once when accompanying a symphonic wind ensemble, I had to play the organ while facing backward—away from the other musicians. Unable to see my face, the conductor had to trust me not to miss my entrances. Meanwhile, I had to trust that the trumpets wouldn't miss their entrance, which gave me the cue for mine. The trumpets, in turn, were relying on the flutes, who were listening to the percussionists, who were counting diligently under their breath.

A symphony is a massive exercise in trust.

Pistis also refers to "trustfulness," the tendency to trust and believe.[10] This is what 1 Corinthians 13:7 means when it says that love "believes all things" and "hopes all things." While we should be discerning, our default should be to rely on one another. As leaders, we have to trust our choirs, band members, and audiovisual technicians to be prepared. We also have to trust our congregations to participate because, otherwise, our job is just awkward. As laypeople, we have to trust our leaders to choose fitting music. We also have to trust those around us to sing with us and not to make us self-conscious.

Corporate worship is an exercise in mutual trust.

Faithfulness and Musicianship Thrive in the Ordinary and Mundane

After performing my final recital in college, I thought I'd be happy. I wasn't. Once I was not held to a practice regimen, instead of feeling liberated, I felt unmoored. Whereas long days of practicing left me tired but satisfied, that short hour in the spotlight—supposedly my crowning achievement—let me down. Performing did not shape my character in the way that the daily practicing did.

While we should be bold about our faith, faithfulness is often cultivated in privacy and mundanity. It is planted in small,

10 Marvin R. Vincent, *Word Studies in the New Testament*, vol. 4 (Charles Scribner's Sons, 1887), 168.

everyday practices, and tended through tiny, seemingly insignificant tasks. But an ordinary, reliable life is worth more than a few shining moments. God sees not just our time in the spotlight but our steady work behind the scenes and promises that such faithfulness will be awarded a "crown of righteousness" (2 Tim. 4:8).

Closing Hymn: "Take My Life and Let It Be"

This hymn is also known as the "consecration hymn." Its author, Frances Havergal (1836–1879), died at only forty-two years old after suffering poor health throughout her life. She was a passionate evangelist, an exceptional vocalist, and a prolific hymn writer. She even left a career as a concert musician to sing only sacred music, true to the third verse of this hymn. Havergal beautifully reflected the steadfastness of her Lord as she maintained hope and integrity through sickness and health, wealth and poverty, fame and anonymity.[11]

The first three verses of "Take My Life and Let It Be" ask the Lord to use every moment, every day, every ability, and even every part of our bodies for his glory. As we read the words of this song, may we likewise consecrate every facet of our lives to the Lord. May we take our ministries day by day. May our hands practice diligently and play skillfully. May our voices raise this constant refrain: God is faithful.

Take my life and let it be
Consecrated, Lord, to thee.
Take my moments and my days;

11 Leland Ryken, *40 Favorite Hymns on the Christian Life: A Closer Look at Their Spiritual and Poetic Meaning* (P&R, 2019), 122–23.

Let them flow in endless praise,
Let them flow in endless praise.

Take my hands and let them move
At the impulse of thy love.
Take my feet and let them be
Swift and beautiful for thee,
Swift and beautiful for thee.

Take my voice and let me sing
Always, only, for my King.
Take my lips and let them be
Filled with messages from thee,
Filled with messages from thee.

Take my silver and my gold;
Not a mite would I withhold.
Take my intellect and use
Every power as thou shalt choose,
Every power as thou shalt choose.

Take my will and make it thine;
It shall be no longer mine.
Take my heart, it is thine own;
It shall be thy royal throne,
It shall be thy royal throne.

Take my love; my Lord, I pour
At thy feet its treasure store.

Take myself, and I will be
Ever, only, all for thee,
Ever, only, all for thee.[12]

Reflection/Discussion

1. Describe a time you had to worship in awkward or adverse circumstances. What did this experience teach you?

2. Who on your team do you trust to always be prepared? Thank that person for his or her faithfulness.

3. Are you balancing diligent work and confident rest? How or how not?

4. What looming task do you need to take "note by note" this week? How can you split it up into manageable pieces?

5. What role models do you want to emulate in your life and worship?

12 Frances Havergal, "Take My Life, and Let It Be," Hymnary.org, 1874, https://hymnary.org/.

8

Gentleness

Becoming Worship Servants

Put on then, as God's chosen ones, holy and beloved, compassionate hearts, kindness, humility, meekness, and patience.

COLOSSIANS 3:12

ONE CHRISTMAS EVE early in my ministry, a teenage vocalist was scheduled to sing "O Holy Night." Now, this song is not for the faint-hearted. On top of some understandable nervousness, this student had a nasty cold. Still, she didn't want to quit. This was one of her first forays into worship leadership, and she wanted to see it through.

But those high notes had other plans, and the sound check was rough.

Our director could have told the student to try again next year and sung the solo herself. An established worship leader and classically trained soprano, she would have had no trouble doing so. But she did not dismiss or replace the young singer. Instead, she sang with her. The two voices blended better than I expected. Why? Because our director held back. She used her voice to support, not overpower, her student's. When they reached the high notes, the leader's subdued presence was enough to bolster her student's confidence, seeing her safely through the treacherous passage.

That impromptu duet resounded with gentleness as a healthy voice strengthened a sick one, a professional vocalist encouraged a student singer, and a confident leader accompanied a tremulous volunteer.

The Formational Fruit

"Gentleness" (*prautēs*) in Galatians 5:23 is "the quality of not being overly impressed by a sense of one's self-importance."[1] Synonyms include *humility*, *modesty*, and *meekness*. To our ears, "meekness" may seem synonymous with timidity or even incompetence, but the older meaning is highly favorable. It was used to describe a king who wielded his authority not to dominate but to care for his subjects.[2] Just as modesty does not necessarily refer to poverty or ugliness but humility and sensitivity, meekness is not powerlessness but power under control.

Does this sound familiar? Our King is likewise powerful and gentle. In Matthew 11:28–30, Jesus invites weary souls to come to

1 Frederick William Danker, ed., *A Greek-English Lexicon of the New Testament and Other Early Christian Literature*, 3rd ed. (University of Chicago Press, 2000), 861; hereafter, BDAG.

2 BDAG 861.

him for rest and describes himself as "gentle and lowly in heart." Author and pastor Dane Ortlund writes, "In the one place in the Bible where the Son of God pulls back the veil and lets us peer way down into the core of who he is . . . his surprising claim is that he is 'gentle and lowly in heart.' "[3] The heart of our Savior is perfect gentleness, but his meekness is not weakness. Jesus invites us to come to him for care and comfort. But this invitation would be empty if he did not also have the power to save and protect us. Christ is our good shepherd, and let's not forget that shepherds both tended their sheep gently and guarded them fiercely.

Jesus is gentle with us, offering rest and restoration from his very heart. When we live and sing in gentleness, we are formed more and more in the likeness of Christ. Gentle worship is worship after Christ's own heart. It is not weak or incompetent but willingly humble, modest, and others-oriented.

Servants of Worship

At the church where I work, staff and volunteers are called "servants of worship." This is no arbitrary choice of wording; it's a statement about the identity and role of Christian leaders. Jesus taught his disciples to reject honorifics such as "rabbi" or "instructor" because they might lend themselves to arrogance (Matt. 23:8–12). While we do not need to reject our job titles (this would generate more confusion than humility), we do need to think of ourselves, first and foremost, as servants.

In Mark 10:36–45, James and John ask Jesus to let them sit beside him in glory. Jesus replies, "You do not know what you are

3 Dane Ortlund, *Gentle and Lowly: The Heart of Christ for Sinners and Sufferers* (Crossway, 2020), 18.

asking. Are you able to drink the cup that I drink, or to be baptized with the baptism with which I am baptized?" (10:38). The bombastic "sons of thunder" mistake self-promotion as the path to glory, but Jesus sorrowfully tells them that it is self-sacrifice.

When the other disciples learn of this conversation, they are less than thrilled with James and John. It seems they want that position of honor for themselves. Again, Jesus corrects them:

> You know that those who are considered rulers of the Gentiles lord it over them, and their great ones exercise authority over them. But it shall not be so among you. But whoever would be great among you must be your servant, and whoever would be first among you must be slave of all. For even the Son of Man came not to be served but to serve, and to give his life as a ransom for many. (Mark 10:42–45)

The world pursues glory by grabbing power and ruling with an iron fist, but our glory as Christians is to be formed in the likeness of our humble, sacrificial Savior. Gentleness must be our greatness. Service must be our success.

Theologian Francis Schaeffer writes that "to do the Lord's work in the Lord's way, we must take Jesus's teaching seriously: he does not want us to press on to the greatest place unless he himself makes it impossible to do otherwise."[4] Whether we are a director in a large church, a part-time leader, a volunteer, or a layperson, we should all desire the same thing: to do the Lord's work in the Lord's way. And we should all seek to reflect "the mentality of

4 Francis A. Schaeffer, *The Lord's Work in the Lord's Way*, in "*The Lord's Work in the Lord's Way*" and "*No Little People*," Crossway Short Classics (Crossway, 2022), 43.

Christ who humbled himself even to death on a cross" by willingly taking the lower place.[5] This humility is the heart of worship, the heart of gentleness, and the heart of Jesus who took on the form of a servant in relentless pursuit of the Father's will (John 6:38).

If we refuse to serve in humility, we have no business reaching for power. God may raise us into positions of greater authority; that's his prerogative. He may also protect or discipline us by keeping us in lower positions. In either case, our job is to do our duty as servants (Luke 17:10). If this sounds like drudgery, take heart: God loves the lowly. As Mary's song proclaims, God scatters the proud but—whether in this life or the next—he exalts the humble (1:51–52).

Gentle Leadership

It would be silly for worship leaders to never lead a new song, never make decisions, or never take initiative. Gentleness does not mean we become bad leaders. Instead, it forms us for Christlike servant-leadership as described in Philippians 2:5–11:

> Have this mind among yourselves, which is yours in Christ Jesus, who, though he was in the form of God, did not count equality with God a thing to be grasped, but emptied himself, by taking the form of a servant, being born in the likeness of men. And being found in human form, he humbled himself by becoming obedient to the point of death, even death on a cross. Therefore God has highly exalted him and bestowed on him the name that is above every name, so that at the name

5 Schaeffer, *Lord's Work*, 43.

> of Jesus every knee should bow, in heaven and on earth and under the earth, and every tongue confess that Jesus Christ is Lord, to the glory of God the Father.

This call to humility is rooted in union with Christ. We are to have the mind of Christ—to think like Jesus. And you know what Jesus seemed to think about most often? The glory of his Father and the well-being of his sheep. Let's consider three ways we as leaders ought to be conformed to the mind and heart of Christ.

First, *gentle leaders serve*. Philippians confronts us with the astonishing fact that the Son of God took on the form of a servant. Who are we, then, to bypass service for leadership? It is healthy for ourselves and our churches that so many of us began leading worship as volunteers. While Scripture is clear that vocational leaders deserve fair wages and respect, learning to sacrifice our time and energy as volunteers first helps instill in us the awareness that worship is not about our gain or glory.

Second, *gentle leaders support*. While Philippians gives us a glimpse of Jesus the roaring, triumphant lion, it also describes him as the sacrificial Lamb who looked to the interests of the lowly. On a far smaller scale, we can look to the interests of others by letting them plan or lead when appropriate. We do not need to insist on our own authority when others with experience and expertise are present. For example, while I am the director of my church choir, many of my singers have been serving in worship longer than I have. By accepting and applying their input, I am learning not only gentleness but love, which "does not insist on its own way" (1 Cor. 13:5). If we are unwilling to worship in the background, we probably have no business taking the foreground.

We need not be territorial of center stage. We should be eager to see others rise and flourish.

Third, *gentle leaders submit.* Scripture reveals that the Son of God is God. It also tells us that Jesus submitted to the Father and learned obedience (Heb. 5:8). If the Son of God did not scorn submission, then neither should we. In my current position, I know that the elders would confront me if I abandoned biblical principles in my worship or life. I've found that such discipline is sadly rare. If you want to play music without constraints, plenty of churches would love to benefit from your skill while neglecting your soul. But I implore you to place yourself under biblical authorities who will hold you accountable and to whom you will submit.

Before you feel too beaten down, remember that Philippians 2:3–11 ends with Christ's exaltation. In the words of the Puritan prayer, "The Valley of Vision": "The way down is the way up . . . to be low is to be high . . . to bear the cross is to wear the crown."[6] Humble service paves the way for tremendous blessing, in eternity and on earth. Let's now consider two practical outworkings of gentle leadership.

First, *gentle leadership protects your witness.* When you serve readily, charges of pride or ambition aren't likely to stick. When you allow others to take more prominent roles, you are less open to accusations of self-centeredness or of making worship your own personal concert. When you submit to biblical authority, you establish guardrails to protect your character, reputation, and ministry. When you are known for treating those around you with

6 Arthur Bennett, "The Valley of Vision," in *The Valley of Vision: A Collection of Puritan Prayers and Devotions* (Banner of Truth, 1975), xxiv–xxv.

tenderness and having their best in mind, you will be better poised to take strong stances or make difficult decisions when necessary.

Second, *gentle leadership promotes others' worship*. Have you ever attended a church where something about the worship leader made it difficult to focus and participate? Perhaps something about his or her attitude didn't quite smell of humility. Arrogant or abrasive leaders may short-circuit their people's praise, but gentle leaders are conduits. Think about it acoustically: Sound is absorbed by some surfaces (such as carpet or foam panels) but reflected by others (such as concrete or the smooth stone of cathedrals). We ought to be like sound-enhancing surfaces. Our job isn't to soak up our people's praise for ourselves but to let it bounce off us, reverberating outward and rising heavenward.

A Note on Modesty

Because it is a potential synonym for gentleness, it is worth briefly addressing modesty. One of my choir directors used to say, "We hear with our eyes." While music is primarily auditory, our senses cannot be parsed out as neatly as we might think. Music (when made in person) is also a visual experience. This is why ensembles wear uniforms; cohesive attire minimizes distractions and supports a unified sound.

Our primary calling as worship leaders is to direct attention to the Lord, but at the same time our ministry often requires us to be highly visible. This poses a unique challenge. While I am not advocating for choir robes or strict uniforms, modesty invites us to pay attention to our attire and composure. We should seek to present ourselves respectably, that is, tidily, appropriately, and suited to our particular churches. There is a wide spectrum here based on cultural and demographic factors, but the undergirding principle should be the same. For instance, because I lead traditional worship, it is not unusual for me to wear a suit, but if my husband wears one to our more contemporary services, people will ask him who died.

Similarly, consider your movements and expressions while leading. Do these set the tone for or distract from your congregation's worship? Again, this will vary based on the temperament of your congregation. If I threw my hands up and began swaying during my traditional service, it would get awkward real fast, but that might be the norm at your church—and that's wonderful.

Ultimately, modesty is a posture of the heart more than a feature of fashion, but this makes it more, not less, significant. When we stand before our churches, our attitude, actions, and attire should proclaim with John the Baptist, "He must increase, but I must decrease" (John 3:30).

Gentle Participation

Gentleness is not limited to leaders. Because all Christians are called to serve the Lord and one another in worship, gentleness must also inform our engagement as participants. Imagine this familiar scene: You're singing with your church family, enjoying worship and fellowship until, suddenly, your ears begin to prickle, tuning to one voice that refuses to blend and rises above dozens of others. We have probably all encountered this sort of singer. He (or she) is *very* pleased by his voice and knows nobody will confront him about his tendency to show off. "Aren't we *supposed* to sing with our *whole* hearts?" you can practically hear him replying.

Our whole hearts, yes. But our whole voices? Not always—not when our lack of humility overpowers and distracts others.

The pattern for church life throughout the New Testament is that of the strong serving the weak. This goes for voices as well. If you have the resonance of an opera singer, corporate worship may be an opportunity for you to practice mutual submission by exercising vocal control. Even as a participant, you can make corporate worship too much about yourself.

Such vanity also rears its ugly head in stubbornness. The singer who loves to show off his voice is often accompanied by the non-singer who loves to showcase her opinions. (I admit that I have been this person.) This individual makes worship about herself by adamantly *not* participating. Clamped jaws and crossed arms demonstrate her disdain for a particular song, style, or singer. Even if you cannot sing certain songs on grounds of conscience, this does not negate your obligation to gentleness. Refrain respectfully if you must, but don't be like a Pharisee, flaunting your "righteousness" while neglecting humility.

Bonhoeffer states bluntly, "There is no place in the service of worship where vanity and bad taste can so intrude as in the singing."[7] Don't be what he calls a "destroyer" of unified singing. You may not be onstage, but you must be on guard. Sing with gusto, but—more importantly—sing with gentleness.

Gentle Singers, Gentle Songs

Prautēs ("gentle" or "meek") is used not only to describe people but also things such as light, wind, and *sound*.[8] Our music itself

7 Dietrich Bonhoeffer, *Life Together: The Classic Exploration of Christian Community*, trans. John W. Doberstein (HarperOne, 1954), 60.

8 Marvin R. Vincent, *Word Studies in the New Testament*, vol. 1 (Charles Scribner's Sons, 1887), 37.

should testify to the heart and mind of our Savior. Like our singers, our songs must be gentle.

In chapter 3, we considered how individuals with certain disabilities or disorders may be unintentionally excluded from our worship. While we need not be legalistic about dramatic worship styles, we must be willing to temper them with gentleness. If we find that our audiovisual effects are regularly barring Christians with health or sensory issues from participating, we risk amputating a member of the body of Christ—a member in need of tender care. It's hard to believe this would not grieve our compassionate Savior to the core.

We also need to pay attention to musical details that are not necessarily health concerns. Like medicine, the goal of gentle worship is not merely to "do no harm" but to *be of help*. Throughout my time in worship ministry, I've noticed the decline of two important things: music literacy and vocal range. Fewer and fewer people can read music, and many songs are too high for laypeople to sing comfortably. My first reaction to these realizations was indignance; I wished people would learn to read music, pick out harmonies, or work on their vocal health. But gentleness compels me to take responsibility and to find ways to mitigate these issues.

I cannot rewrite the hymnal or give voice lessons to my entire congregation, but I can transpose songs down when possible and resist the urge to modulate to higher keys. Contemporary leaders may likewise consider lowering their songs a step or two and highlighting harmonies for participants to follow. A weakness that all leaders may need to combat is the tendency to amplify ourselves and our teams to the point that our people cannot hear themselves.

Pastor and author Tim Challies writes, "The most successful worship leaders are the ones who want to hear their congregations sing . . . the ones most attuned to the musical ability of their congregations and the ones most committed to choosing songs their people can sing."[9] Gentleness calls us to make every effort to help our people participate even when it means we must become less. At the end of the day, doesn't it seem fitting that this humility may lead us to literally lower our pitch or volume?

We should also be sensitive to one another's unique learning styles and backgrounds. As a visual and textual learner, I love poetry and can read most church music on sight. Meanwhile, my brother, an aural and kinesthetic learner, learns by hearing and doing. Christians like him may sing with less anxiety when songs are more straightforward and repetitive. Recognizing this diversity of learning styles has helped me program a better variety of music and has softened how I interact with those who process information differently than I do.

In the same way, rather than making assumptions about others based on their musical preferences, we should seek to understand why they hold those preferences. One worshiper may crave simple choruses because she grew up in a culture of extrabiblical legalism, and these remind her of God's grace. Another may relish ancient anthems because they help him connect to our historic faith amid a rapidly changing society. Being aware of the baggage people bring with them to worship can help us treat one another (and one another's music) with compassion.

While musical worship is primarily for the church and not the world, this does include newer believers. We must take care that our songs do not become status symbols composed exclusively of highbrow language or complicated melodies. In grad school,

9 Tim Challies, "The Mark of the Most Successful Worship Leaders," *Challies.com* (blog), August 9, 2017, https://www.challies.com/.

I jokingly wrote a Christmas carol using purely academic language. It was completely unintelligible, but that was the point of the joke: Inaccessibility does not equal depth. At the same time, gentleness does not require us to dispose of intricate composition and theological language. (Through hymns, I learned wonderful words like *diadem* and *paraclete*.) Instead, we can enjoy a balance of songs that all Christians can sing with confidence and those that will increase our knowledge and capabilities. We may be able to explain complex lyrics or pair complicated songs with simpler choruses. In these ways, gentle worship—like our gentle Savior—meets us where we are but does not leave us as we were.

Bonhoeffer asserts that "the elimination of the weak is the death of fellowship."[10] Excluding those we see as weaker than us threatens truly corporate worship. Because we are united in Christ, excluding Christians who require gentler (or just different) treatment is severing parts of our own body (1 Cor. 12:14–27). Moreover, it is rejecting opportunities to be conformed to Christ, who had compassion on the injured and ignored. As we champion our congregations' understanding, musicality, and giftedness, let's first seek to be, like David, singers after God's own heart (1 Sam. 13:14).

Musicianship and Meekness

In a celebrity culture, we don't often associate musicianship with modesty or humility. Even the title "worship leader" may conjure images of stages, stylish outfits, and spotlights. And yet, when we keep our eyes on Christ, our music-making can foster gentleness, humility, and modesty in the following unique ways.

10 Bonhoeffer, *Life Together*, 94.

Mastery Should Breed Meekness

Surprisingly, the most accomplished musicians I've known are also the humblest. Meanwhile, I've found that less competent musicians are often more prone to pride. This phenomenon is known as the Dunning-Kruger effect. Basically, inexperienced individuals overestimate their abilities because they are not proficient enough to recognize their deficiencies. They don't know what they don't know. Conversely, highly competent individuals downplay their abilities because as their knowledge increases, so does their self-awareness.[11] They know how hard they have had to work and how far they have yet to go.

"Who is wise and understanding among you? By his good conduct let him show his works in the meekness of wisdom" (James 3:13). The wiser we are, the humbler we ought to be. This seems topsy-turvy, but that's how gentleness rolls: The truly wise are gentle, and the best leaders serve. The further we get in our ministries, the more competent *and* the more humble we should be. Indeed, we should keep learning and growing as a means of staying humble since the more you know, the more you know you don't know—you know? As our maturity and wisdom increase, our estimation of ourselves should decrease. For Christians, there ought to be an inverse relationship between accomplishment and arrogance.

Service Requires Skill

When playing duets with my piano students, I follow them—not because they are in charge, but because I can adapt to their

11 Shishira Sreenivas and Shawna Seed, "The Dunning-Kruger Effect: Causes, Examples, and Impact," *WebMD*, February 7, 2024, https://www.webmd.com/.

wayward tempos. Unable to regulate their rhythms, my littlest students can only lead, but I am skilled enough to serve. Many musicians can play flawless solos but—whether due to ability or attitude—cannot collaborate with others. They are great enough to be soloists but not servants. I used to have the skewed idea that worship ministry was a fallback for musicians who did not make it as performers, but this is far from true. Instead, musicians called to worship leadership are those skilled enough to perform and humble enough to serve.

Two of my own piano teachers were the top-ranked pianists in their home country, yet they spent much of their time praying for their students. I marvel at the director at my first job, who performed internationally and led a choir of retired volunteers with equal diligence. I think of my organ teacher in Scotland, who was content to write beautiful music for his church apart from publication or profit. To wholeheartedly accept "the lower place" of music ministry when one could pursue a more glamorous career (in the world's eyes) requires true gentleness—power under control.

Thorns Keep Us Humble

As I mentioned in chapter 6, I struggle with performance anxiety, but this weakness keeps me from relying on my efforts and abilities. I pray often that God would remove my fear. Sometimes he does; sometimes he doesn't. Most often, he lets me play well externally even though I am quaking internally.

In 2 Corinthians 12:1–10, Paul writes about seeing divine, inexpressible glory. Interestingly, he writes about this experience as if it happened to another man, making it clear that he is not boasting of his achievements but of God's grace. The closest Paul comes to bragging about himself in this passage is when he mentions his "thorn in the flesh." The same gracious God who gives Paul a vision of glory permits the thorn to remain despite his repeated prayers for its removal. A few chapters earlier, Paul writes, "Let the one who boasts, boast in the Lord" (2 Cor. 10:17). This is the point of thorns. They bring us low to remind us of who is on high.

While they might detract from certain aspects of our skill, our weaknesses or pain points may position us to be better worshipers. Perhaps there's an attendee who never fails to point out your missed notes. Or you cringe whenever you hear your voice in recordings. Maybe you can't read music swiftly or transpose on sight. Perhaps you're prone to sore throats or arthritis, making your vocation physically painful. In any case, I hope you'll take comfort from the fact that just as God disciplines those he loves, he permits thorns to keep his chosen leaders humble.

Submission Is a Prerequisite

Watch any good ensemble, and you'll see submission in action as musicians give and take, listen and respond. Meanwhile, bad ensembles typically suffer from a lack of submission. Harmonic balance is nonexistent as singers battle for attention, tuning is absent as string players depend on personal ideas of pitch, and cohesion vanishes as the conductor waves his baton futilely. The worst choir I ever heard did not lack ability; its members simply disregarded all authority.

In Ephesians 5, being filled with the Spirit gives rise to corporate singing and mutual submission (Eph. 5:18–21). Moreover, singing together is a way of practicing such submission. Steven Guthrie writes that singing fosters submission because it "involves synchronicity—staying in time with one another. The singers submit themselves to a common tempo, a common musical structure and rhythm."[12] When we gather to sing, we must also come ready to submit—to be formed in Christlikeness as we participate in something bigger than ourselves and look to the interests of others over ourselves.

Closing Hymn: "May the Mind of Christ, My Savior"

Little is known about Kate Barclay Wilkinson (1859–1928), the author of this hymn. How fitting for a song about humble service! The first verse draws on Philippians 2:5. The second verse expands on this, emphasizing that to live according to the mind of Christ, we need to let his word permeate our hearts. When our minds and hearts are conformed to Christ, we are prepared to tend to the weakest among us, as described in the third verse. In all this, we magnify our servant-king, whose upside-down path brings victory.

The fifth verse offers a contrast to the others as it suddenly turns from meekness to determination. But these are not so different as they may at first seem. Gentleness requires true strength—the power found only in Christ and shared with us by the Spirit. The final verse captures the goal of gentleness: to make and mature disciples by making known the heart of Christ.

> May the mind of Christ, my Savior,
> Live in me from day to day,

12 Steven R. Guthrie, "The Wisdom of Song," in *Resonant Witness: Conversations Between Music and Theology*, ed. Jeremy S. Begbie and Steven R. Guthrie (Eerdmans, 2011), 401.

By his love and pow'r controlling
All I do and say.

May the word of God dwell richly
In my heart from hour to hour,
So that all may see I triumph
Only through his pow'r.

May the peace of God my Father
Rule my life in everything,
That I may be calm to comfort
Sick and sorrowing.

May the love of Jesus fill me
As the waters fill the sea;
Him exalting, self abasing:
This is victory.

May I run the race before me,
Strong and brave to face the foe,
Looking only unto Jesus
As I onward go.

May His beauty rest upon me
As I seek the lost to win,
And may they forget the channel,
Seeing only him.[13]

13 Kate B. Wilkinson, "May the Mind of Christ, My Savior," Hymnary.org, 1925, https://hymnary.org/.

Reflection/Discussion

1. How has volunteering shaped your approach to musical worship?

2. Can you think of a time you made worship too much about yourself?

3. Have you ever felt excluded from corporate worship based on ability or learning style? Are there any ways you may be unintentionally excluding other Christians?

4. Do you agree that the more competent you are, the humbler you should become? Why or why not?

5. What "thorn" is the Lord permitting to keep you humble?

9

Self-Control

Practicing Freedom

Every athlete exercises self-control in all things. They do it to receive a perishable wreath, but we an imperishable.

1 CORINTHIANS 9:25

I RECENTLY LEARNED a piece that was meant to be played "with abandon." Ironically, it took quite a bit of practice. First, I had to play "with focus" and "with a metronome."

I had to practice with self-control to play "with abandon."

Scripture employs athletic imagery to depict self-control, but practicing music provides a similarly apt analogy. Like athletes, serious musicians learn to exercise restraint in "all things." When preparing for recitals or competitions, I avoided anything that could injure my hands—such as rollerblading and trampolines (although I ended up breaking my arm while making coffee).

Before concerts, my choir directors enforced strict "no dairy" policies to keep our voices clear. The perpetual refrain among my peers in college was, "I can't. I have to practice."

This life of restraint, however, is not without its reward. The musicians I know who play and sing with the greatest ease are those who dedicated years to the most intense discipline. So, too, if we want to worship with freedom—with clarity, readiness, and longevity—we must learn to approach musical worship with sober minds, pure hearts, and disciplined bodies.

The Fasting Fruit

To exercise self-control (*enkrateia*) is to hold dominion over ourselves by ruling over our emotions, impulses, and desires.[1] Self-control does not mean that we lack passion or desire—nobody wants an indifferent worship leader, after all—but that we are not ruled by these. We must be able to regulate our impulses and balance our emotions. This coincides with another translation of *enkrateia*: "temperance," the avoidance of extremes.[2]

Temperance is also "the virtue of one who masters . . . his sensual appetites."[3] "Appetites" refers to all fleshly desires, but its immediate association with food is insightful. Self-control is inextricable from fasting, which typically has to do with abstaining from food to focus on a higher goal—such as serving the Lord. It's no coincidence that fasting and worship often go

1 Frederick William Danker, ed., *A Greek-English Lexicon of the New Testament and Other Early Christian Literature*, 3rd ed. (University of Chicago Press, 2000), 274; hereafter, BDAG.

2 Joseph H. Thayer, *Thayer's Greek-English Lexicon of the New Testament* (1889; repr., Hendrickson, 2023), 166–67.

3 Thayer, *Greek-English Lexicon*, 166–67.

together in Scripture (Luke 2:37; Acts 13:2). Both call us to set aside distractions and to refocus our minds, hearts, and bodies on serving the Lord. Both call us to exercise self-control in "all things," to bear this fruit of the Spirit mentally, emotionally, and physically (1 Cor. 9:25).

Self-control is the "fasting fruit." It requires us to forgo anything that might distract from our worship—even things that are not overtly wrong. Just as elite athletes must evaluate every decision according to the question "Will this help me win?," self-control challenges us to weigh every habit, yearning, attitude, effect, and song against the ultimate question: "Will this help *our worship*?" (Hint: If the answer is no, the thing must go.)

The good news in all this is that we fast so we can feast. As the great Puritan pastor Jonathan Edwards writes, "There is no such virtue as temperance in spiritual feasting."[4] When we abstain from things that might hinder our worship, it is only so that we can worship to the fullest. There is no such thing as too much worship.

The Final Fruit

The nature of self-control as the fasting fruit may provide a clue as to why it is listed last in Galatians 5:22–23. Whereas the fruit of the Spirit is rooted in love, it is pruned via self-control. As one pastor puts it:

> It should be no surprise Paul ends his list of the fruit of the Spirit with self-control. . . . Paul wants us to get to work. Whatever is keeping us from loving others or being gentle must be put to

4 Jonathan Edwards, *The Works of Jonathan Edwards*, vol. 14, *Sermons and Discourses: 1723–1729*, ed. Kenneth P. Minkema (Yale University Press, 1997), 286.

> death. But the desires of the flesh won't go down without a fight. Walking in love and joy won't be easy. We need self-control.[5]

It is impossible to imagine a peaceful or patient person who lacks self-control. We cannot treat one another with kindness or goodness without overcoming our selfishness. The steadiness of faithfulness and the discipline of self-control go hand in hand. Gentleness quietly demands that we temper our passions.

As love gives root to each subsequent fruit, self-control weeds out anything that may diminish our fruitfulness and detract from our worship. Together, they bookend the fruit of the Spirit as love gives life and self-control removes what is dead.

Spirit-Control

With its emphasis on the self, self-control may sound discouraging. How many of us feel capable of complete control of ourselves? Thankfully, just as God did not leave Adam to exercise dominion over creation alone but provided Eve as a helper, we practice this "dominion of self" by the power of the Holy Spirit—*the* Helper (Gen. 2:18; John 14:16). Self-control comes from within ourselves, but it is not purely of ourselves. It is the work of the Spirit, killing off and cutting out the remains of our fleshly ways, exposing and excising anything that might strangle our singing. "Self-control" is thus an ironic translation, for it is ultimately about being controlled by the Spirit and putting off our old selves (Col. 3:5–10).

Here is some further good news: Singing together is a way to practice self-control as "Spirit-control." Let's return to two of this

5 Aaron Menikoff, "The Flesh Is Weak: Pastoral Reflections on Self-Control," 9Marks, November 16, 2017, https://www.9marks.org/.

book's core texts. Colossians 3:5–17 is all about putting on the new self, and it culminates in a call to sing together. When we gather to sing, we at once reject our old way of life and reinforce our new identity in Christ. But how? Ephesians 5:1–21 suggests that singing together not only results from being filled with the Spirit but is a means of being filled with the Spirit. Elsewhere in Scripture "filled with the Spirit" describes a state of being or an act of God. Here, it is a command, and it is coupled with a call to song. We receive the Spirit when we come to Christ, but Ephesians commands us to keep on being filled as we keep on singing.

This continuous filling produces self-control. Like a glass that is so full of water it cannot contain anything else, the more filled we are with the Spirit, the less we will seek satisfaction elsewhere.[6] Thus, it is not human fasting but the Spirit's filling that empowers our self-control. We abstain from the sins of the old self not by willfully remaining empty but by constantly seeking the Spirit's fullness. And isn't it marvelous that God lets us develop such self-control not merely by avoiding sin but by adding more singing?

Sober Singing

Peter writes, "Be self-controlled and sober-minded for the sake of your prayers" (1 Pet. 4:7). Likewise, we must be self-controlled and sober-minded for the sake of our worship.

While the type of singing prescribed by Ephesians 5:18–21 is a means of exercising self-control, this does not mean that all singing is self-controlled. We see in this passage that being filled with the Spirit replaces being filled with wine, and singing replaces

6 Thomas A. Tarrants, "Finding Power to Live a New Life: Discipleship and the Holy Spirit," *C. S. Lewis Institute* (blog), March 4, 2012, https://www.cslewisinstitute.org/.

debauchery. But not just any singing will do. The drunken debauchery here is an intoxication that results in a complete loss of inhibition. Such a state could easily lead to unwise speech and riotous singing.[7] Thus, the contrast here is not simply between singing and sinning, but between two types of singing: intelligible, intentional worship and inebriated noise.

The contrast between drunkenness and the Holy Spirit is a theme throughout the New Testament. At Pentecost, witnesses cannot fathom that the disciples' fervor is not caused by "new wine" (Acts 2:13). But this "new wine"—the Holy Spirit—brings clarity rather than chaos (Luke 5:37–38). Instead of slurred speech or mindless babbling, the Spirit empowers the disciples to share the gospel with a multitude of people in a multitude of languages rationally and joyfully. Likewise, when we gather to sing, we must be careful to do so in an intentional, orderly, reasonable manner. Our singing must be sober. Spirit-filled singing must replace *spirits*-filled singing. The first proceeds from and reinforces the ministry of the Holy Spirit, who empowers self-control. The latter is stimulated by excess alcohol, which causes a loss of control.

Ancient pagan worship often involved substances and altered mental states. By contrast, faithful Jewish prophets and, later, Christian teachers abstained from strong drink to keep "distinct before the world the ecstasy caused by the Spirit, from that caused by wine."[8] In the same way, when we worship with sober minds, we prove that our enthusiasm is not that of

7 BDAG 625.

8 Robert Jamieson, A. R. Fausset, and David Brown, *Commentary Critical and Explanatory on the Whole Bible*, Christian Classics Ethereal Library, 1871, https://ccel.org/.

drunkenness but true understanding and thankfulness. Sober singing testifies to the Spirit's power in our lives. Our minds are clear and our joy is genuine. We know what we are doing. We know who we are worshiping. When we prioritize sobriety, we worship without disruption and witness to the world that we are filled with something better than any substance: the "new wine" promised by Jesus, the Spirit of "power and love and self-control" (2 Tim. 1:7).

Before we congratulate ourselves for sipping only coffee during worship, let's remember that drunkenness is not the only form of insobriety. Bitterness is blinding. Secret sin skews our perception. Anger and arrogance are intoxicating. A critical spirit distorts right judgment. Even highly expressive music can be confusing if not coupled with intelligible lyrics. Elaborate effects may become distracting if their purpose cannot be explained. We must examine ourselves and our worship, and be willing to reevaluate anything that does not foster focused participation.

We must learn to set aside anything—even good things—that might obstruct clear-minded worship. As we praise with our spirit, we must also sing with our minds (1 Cor. 14:15). Like soldiers who used to tie up their robes to run freely, sober singing charges us to "gird up the loins of [our minds]" (1 Pet. 1:13 KJV). We must combat any distracted or distorted thinking that may cause us to stumble as we sing.

Careful Consumption

The opening lines of Shakespeare's *Twelfth Night* recognize that music feeds and shapes our appetites:

> If music be the food of love, play on.
> Give me an excess of it, that, surfeiting,
> The appetite may sicken, and so die.[9]

Just as the food we eat becomes part of us—the good and the bad—the music we consume soaks into our hearts, shaping our emotions and desires. Self-control invites us to weigh how the music we consume is preparing our hearts for right worship . . . or not.

Unfortunately, just as one salad cannot undo a lifetime of donuts, Sunday worship will do little for our spiritual formation if our daily listening is *de*formative. In a world of fast food, it's easy to eat mindlessly. In this era of streaming, it's easy to listen carelessly. But we must take every thought—and song—captive to Christ (2 Cor. 10:5). We may not need to listen exclusively to worship music, but the songs we play on repeat should reflect whatever is true, honorable, just, pure, lovely, commendable, excellent, and praiseworthy (Phil. 4:8).

Although streaming apps can lead to compulsive consumption, they do provide useful tools for examining our listening habits. If you use Spotify or a similar app, scroll through your personalized playlists. What sort of music does the algorithm think you will consume? What might this say about your heart—your passions and desires? How might you need to adjust your listening habits? How many hours are you streaming music each day? Do you need to "fast" from music to reflect and reset?

9 William Shakespeare, "Twelfth Night; Or, What You Will," in *The Complete Works of William Shakespeare*, The Edition of the Shakespeare Head Press Oxford (Barnes & Noble, 1994), ll. 1–3.

However we enjoy music throughout the week—whether on Spotify, the radio, record players, or at live events—let's take care that the songs we feed our ears and the lyrics we put in our mouths do not take away from our praise (Ps. 40:3).

Technical Training

A crucial component of self-control is control over one's body. The most obvious application of this is that we are to flee bodily sins. Physical self-control, however, is not merely about keeping our bodies from sin but offering them up for righteousness. We are to restrain and train our bodies so we are prepared as "vessels for honorable use" (2 Tim. 2:20–22).

Paul writes, "But I discipline my body and keep it under control, lest after preaching to others I myself should be disqualified" (1 Cor. 9:27). The Greek word for "discipline" in this verse is more severe than in the English. It means to subdue one's body through intense exercise so it is ready to fulfill the task at hand.[10] For athletes, this means eating and working out in order to compete effectively and without injury. For Paul, such discipline involved preparing his body to resist temptation and to withstand hunger, fatigue, persecution, cold, and pain—all while journeying miles upon miles to share the gospel (2 Cor. 11:24–27).

Scripture comforts us that we can worship in our hearts even when our bodies fail—and they will (Eph. 5:19). But, like Paul, our goal should be to equip ourselves for enduring ministry, not only by avoiding disqualifying sin but by adding disciplines that will strengthen and sustain our bodies for our specific callings.

10 Thayer, *Greek-English Lexicon*, 646.

When musicians dedicate themselves to an instrument, their physicality begins to revolve around playing that instrument (or voice, for singers). Have you noticed that musicians often develop physical habits such as stretching their fingers, beating the backs of pews like drums, or practicing chords on air guitars? Piano drills have made me an obnoxiously loud typist, violinists are branded by scars from their chin rests, and classical guitarists can be spotted by their fingernails. Musicians also tend to avoid things that might hinder their physical ability to play or sing well. Singers may trade shouting at events for herbal tea and vocal rest. I avoided sports that could hurt my fingers. A musician's entire way of being embodied is affected by his or her vocation.

For worship musicians, developing and maintaining proper technique is crucial. Have you ever considered that warming up your voice before worship is an act of self-control? Or that practicing scales on the piano is training your hands for service? Or that building up guitar-string callouses is preparing you for lasting ministry? Self-control in "all things" includes such seemingly small things (1 Cor. 9:25).

We should also consider whether there are things and activities we need to limit for the sake of our physical worship. This applies not only to leaders but to laypeople. Perhaps we need to limit caffeine before leading so our tempos don't get out of control. Or maybe we need to stop staying up late on Saturdays so we are rested and punctual on Sundays. Maybe we need to adjust our nutrition and start exercising so we have the stamina to stand and sing more comfortably.

Paul tells Timothy, "While bodily training is of some value, godliness is of value in every way, as it holds promise for the present life and also for the life to come" (1 Tim. 4:8). While the emphasis of this verse is on godliness, let's not gloss over the fact that bodily training is of *some* value. It is not paramount, but it is important. Learning to use our bodies effectively is crucial to our worship and ministry "in this present age." Like athletes, we must steward our bodies to the best of our abilities so that we can endure in physical worship with ease and excellence.

Spontaneous Service

Have you ever watched a top-notch jazz band perform? The musicians improvise and riff off one another with amazing spontaneity. But what audiences hear as unrestrained creativity is the product of rigorous listening, practicing, refining, responding, failing, and fixing. Such hard work may not sound like freedom, but its end product *sounds* free.

I've noticed that many worship leaders tend to equate "Spirit-filled" worship with spontaneous praise. It is a wonderful thing when Christians suddenly burst into song, but—as with a high-quality jazz band—spontaneous music-making is more often the result of years of self-control.

Not convinced? Ask someone who does not know how to play the piano to jump in on keys. Then ask someone who has studied music for decades. Both individuals may be Spirit-filled Christians, but only one is equipped for spontaneous music-making. Self-control prepares us to serve, adapt, and improvise at a moment's notice.

There are two takeaways here: (1) Musical freedom relies on discipline and (2) the end of discipline is *freedom*.

Self-control is connected with staying watchful—with being ready to resist evil and do good at any given moment (1 Pet. 5:8). By keeping our minds clear, our hearts pure, and our bodies under control, we present ourselves to the Lord as ready instruments (Rom. 6:13). For all its emphasis on abstinence, the "fasting fruit" is also the "freedom fruit." It equips us for focused, capable, wholehearted worship—whenever and wherever the Spirit leads.

Music-Making and Self-Control

One of the most profound results of a music education is increased self-control. Perhaps this is another reason why Scripture tells us to cultivate this fruit by singing together regularly. Studying music and participating in corporate worship help us exercise self-control as we manage our time, focus our minds, regulate our emotions, and engage our bodies.

Manage Your Time

Musicians must learn to set aside time for practicing and rehearsing. I have lost count of all the hobbies and outings I have opted out of to protect my practice hours. Even my smallest students are supposed to set aside a bit of time every day to work on their music.

It is no coincidence that Paul tells us to make the best use of our time, and then almost immediately calls us to sing together (Eph. 5:16, 19). While worship leaders and volunteers may not practice for hours every day, they still have to rise early on weekends for band rehearsals or forgo evening commitments to attend choir practice. Even for laypeople, singing together demands our time. It requires us to reschedule other obligations and turn down other opportunities. As with practicing music, saying yes to regular corporate worship requires us to exercise self-control by saying no to other commitments.

Focus Your Mind

I am a chronic multitasker. As a child, my mom caught me reading a novel while practicing my scales. The more advanced I became, though, the more I had to focus on one thing at a time. Every practice session was a chance to hone this focus. I learned to put my phone on airplane mode and lock the studio door in pursuit of one activity—one song, one phrase, one note—at a time.

Worship calls us to fix our minds on Christ (Heb. 12:2). We may still find our fingers twitching toward our phones or our thoughts turning toward our to-do lists, but Sunday keeps coming. Every call to worship is a call to self-control. Every opening song is an invitation to—for at least an hour—turn our thoughts from the distractions and duties of earth and cast our gaze to glory.

Regulate Your Emotions

Music provides a way to express our emotions, as well as to bring them back into balance. If I am grieving, I can sing lament psalms or play a Chopin ballade. At a certain point, though, music-making demands a return to emotional balance or "homeostasis."[11] Diligent musicians must practice their repertoire regardless of how they are feeling, which frequently means playing music that does not match their current state. They learn not only to express their emotions but to channel and redirect them.

11 I owe this term to Professor Marlin Owen.

While our songs should allow space to process complex emotions, the goal is not merely expression but reorientation (see chap. 2). I've begun many rehearsals and services feeling lousy, but singing with other Christians rarely fails to restore my sense of stability. When we join in praise, we are not dismissing our emotions but deciding to work through and rule over them.

Engage Your Body

Music is widely hailed as "the most spiritual of the arts," but it is also inescapably physical.[12] Visit any conservatory of music and you'll see flutists wearing more athletic tape than, well, athletes. The most transcendent music is played on instruments affected by heat and humidity. Our most ephemeral songs proceed from fleshy vocal folds.

Musical worship is a spiritual discipline that largely depends on physical activity. Stand, sit, stand again, clap, sway, inhale, sing. Beyond these basic elements, gathering to sing may mean doing with less sleep, forgoing a workout, or running on half a donut from the lobby. It may mean standing when you're tired, singing when you're groggy, or clapping when you're self-conscious. It means tolerating the various perfumes and personal space issues that come with worshiping together in person. But each time we bring our tired, quirky, aching, noisy bodies to church, we are disciplining them for worship.

Closing Hymn: "Be Thou My Vision"

When struggling with mental focus or emotional balance, I often turn to the hymn "Be Thou My Vision." Each verse is a renewed

12 James MacMillan, *A Scot's Song: A Life of Music* (Birlinn Limited, 2019), 11.

commitment to throwing off sin and distractions in pursuit of clear-sighted, pure-hearted worship. The third verse is perhaps the least popular, but its military imagery drives home the seriousness of self-control; when we gather for worship, we are gearing up for the fight at hand.

As this hymn proclaims, we can count lesser things as "naught," because Christ is our everything (Phil. 3:8–9). It encourages us that, eventually, our fasting will give way to feasting. We exercise self-control here and now in anticipation of the coming kingdom, where rich food, good wine, and extravagant songs will abound forevermore.

Be thou my vision, O Lord of my heart;
Naught be all else to me, save that thou art;
Thou my best thought, by day or by night,
Waking or sleeping, thy presence my light.

Be thou my wisdom, and thou my true Word;
I ever with thee and thou with me, Lord;
Thou my great Father, I thy true son;
Thou in me dwelling, and I with thee one.

Be thou my battle shield, sword for the fight;
Be thou my dignity, thou my delight;
Thou my soul's shelter, thou my high tower;
Raise thou me heav'nward, O pow'r of my pow'r.

Riches I heed not, nor man's empty praise;
Thou mine inheritance, now and always:

Thou and thou only, first in my heart,
High King of Heaven, my treasure thou art.

High King of Heaven, my victory won,
May I reach Heaven's joys, O bright Heaven's Sun!
Heart of my own heart, whatever befall,
Still be my vision, O ruler of all.[13]

Reflection/Discussion

1. How do you see self-control contributing to love, joy, peace, patience, kindness, goodness, faithfulness, and gentleness?

2. Is anything interfering with your ability to worship soberly?

3. What do your listening habits suggest about your desires, passions, and values? Do you need to make any adjustments to foster self-control?

4. Is there anything you can add or avoid this week for the sake of healthy physical worship?

5. Have you experienced the freedom of self-control? In what ways?

13 Mary E. Byrne, trans., "Be Thou My Vision," 1905, versified, Eleanor H. Hull, 1912, Hymnary.org, https://hymnary.org/.

Conclusion

Fruitful Worship

Through him then let us continually offer up a sacrifice of praise to God, that is, the fruit of lips that acknowledge his name.

HEBREWS 13:15

MY FIRST SPRING in Iowa brought daily delights. Every morning when I stepped outside, some new flower or fruit was there to greet me. Born and raised in Arizona, I had no idea one could accidentally grow a mulberry tree. Then suddenly, cherries! Apples! Grapes! Astonished by such abundance, I downloaded a botany app and went plant to plant, finding out what each one was and how to care for it. My cherry tree was thriving, so I picked its fruit and left it alone. My apple tree was dehydrated and growing sideways, so I staked it upright and watered it weekly. My grapevines were taking over, so I pruned them back.

I hope this book has been like that app: helping you identify the fruits that are already flourishing in your worship and discover areas in need of redirection, nourishment, or pruning. I pray that it helps you lead, volunteer, and participate with a revitalized vision of musical worship as a garden ripe for fruitfulness.

Crops and *Karpos*

The word translated as "fruit" (*karpos*) in Galatians 5:22 refers literally to a crop or harvest and figuratively to any result, outcome, or product.[1] What we *do* in worship must glorify God and edify his church. But what we *get out of* our worship—what result or product we hope to yield—must be the increase of spiritual fruit in our lives and the lives of those worshiping with us.

In Scripture's original context, fruitfulness language would have conveyed the extreme urgency and importance of being in Christ and filled with the Spirit. Fruit was central to the diet of the ancient Israelites, cultivated gardens were welcome oases in an unforgiving climate, and fruit was even an acceptable offering to the Lord (Lev. 27:30). Fruit trees were preserved during wars and were part of the appeal of the promised land.[2] May we learn to value the fruit of the Spirit this highly, treating it as essential fuel for the Christian life, a source of refreshment in a challenging world, and a vital characteristic of our worship.

1 Frederick William Danker, ed., *A Greek-English Lexicon of the New Testament and Other Early Christian Literature*, 3rd ed. (University of Chicago Press, 2000), 509–10; hereafter, BDAG.

2 Megan Bishop Moore, "Fruit," in *Eerdman's Dictionary of the Bible*, ed. David Noel Freedman (Eerdmans, 2000), 472–73.

Fruit Loops

Although we have focused on each fruit in turn, *karpos* is a singular term used collectively.[3] We might think of love, joy, peace, patience, kindness, goodness, faithfulness, gentleness, and self-control as distinct fruits from the same harvest or even different flavors of the same fruit. Sinclair Ferguson compares the fruit of the Spirit to a seamless nine-part harmony:

> [Jesus] was able to express all the fruit of the Spirit in a way that must have felt like listening to beautiful voices singing in harmony, weaving in and out of each other to enhance every single voice. . . . When love, joy, and peace sing together, the harmony enhances the quality of each of their voices. And then we can triple that: love, joy, peace, patience, kindness, goodness, faithfulness, gentleness, self-control—three groups singing three-part harmony, uniting together to sing nine-part harmony, heavenly music.[4]

Maintaining this harmony means we can't pick and choose our favorite fruits. We aren't making a fruit salad. Peace cannot exist without patience and gentleness. Trying to experience joy without worshiping faithfully is like playing the lottery. Kindness and goodness are inseparable. Self-control without love becomes pharisaical.

Each fruit should contribute to the others in a productive cycle. We're dealing with fruit loops. As we have seen, love and self-control bookend the fruit, but every fruit has a part to play

3 BDAG 509.

4 Sinclair Ferguson, "The Heavenly Music of Self-Control," Ligonier Ministries, February 23, 2024, https://www.ligonier.org/.

in cultivating the crop as a whole. Faithfulness is steadfast love put into practice. The generosity of goodness evokes joy. Patience and kindness lead to interpersonal peace. Self-control protects gentleness. Pick any two fruits and you'll be able to think of ways they depend on and contribute to each other.

Against Such Things There Is No Law

Galatians 5:22–23 concludes, "Against such things there is no law." Life in the Spirit yields tremendous freedom, in contrast to the condemnation of the law. Indeed, the fruit (namely, love) fulfills the heart of the law (Gal. 5:14).

But what does this mean for musical worship?

The fruit of the Spirit is nonnegotiable, but it is flexible. In our worship, spiritual fruitfulness must be recognizable, but this does not mean rigidity. As long as we are filtering our attitudes, preparation, decisions, participation, and leadership through the lens of fruitfulness, we can adapt our execution to our particular settings and contexts.

Let me offer a simple example. At my first job, I was told to play the hymns slower to help elderly worshipers articulate their words without feeling rushed. At another church, I was asked to play faster so older members could sing full phrases without running out of breath. Both approaches were motivated by gentleness—by a heart for including all participants in worship regardless of age or ability—but the specific outworkings were exactly the opposite. Gentle worship in one church sounded like slower songs and, in another, faster phrases.

Worship characterized by the fruit of the Spirit is like a "theme and variations," a type of composition that takes a melody (the theme) and experiments with it in a multitude of ways (the variations). The melody might be slowed down, sped up, syncopated, or augmented. It might appear in the technicality of a toccata, the playfulness of a scherzo, or the seriousness of a dirge, but it will always be recognizable.

The goal of this book is not to tell you exactly *what* to do in your musical worship but *how* to do it: lovingly, joyfully, peacefully, patiently, kindly, generously, faithfully, gently, and soberly. These fruits might sound different in your church's music than in mine, but the Spirit behind them is the same.

Gardening Tips

I am not a gifted gardener, but I've picked up a few basics. The following principles apply to cultivating both literal and spiritual fruit.

Determine the Kind

I previously assumed there were two types of grapes: red and green. It turns out that this is not the case. To know what fruit to expect from my grapevines and how to increase their harvest, I had to determine what kind I was dealing with.

The first appearance of fruitfulness is in Genesis, where God creates plants, animals, and people, and tells them to be fruitful and multiply after their biological kinds.[5] Oak trees bear acorns. Cats bear kittens. People bear sons and daughters. Christians are to make more Christians. We are to make disciples and grow in Christlikeness—in love, joy, peace, patience, kindness, goodness,

5 BDAG 510.

faithfulness, gentleness, and self-control. We are to bear fruit in keeping with our kind as new creations (Luke 6:43–45; James 3:12). Spirit-filled, fruit-bearing worship is therefore exclusive to Christians. We cannot expect to bear fruit in our worship if we are not first in Christ.

Look to the Vine

My grapevines looked healthy because their branches were taking over my porch, but a friend taught me that the best indicator of their future fruitfulness is the sturdiness and vitality of their central vines. Only the branches connected directly to these survived our ruthless pruning and went on to bear fruit.

Fruitfulness requires us to examine ourselves as branches but, more importantly, to focus on the life and health of our true vine. When we take our eyes off Christ, we are prone to become all leaves and no grapes. Apart from Christ, our trappings of productivity and artistry can bear no fruit; but the more we focus our lives and worship on Christ, the more readily we will bear fruit in keeping with his character (John 15:1–7).

Prune Intensely

Pruning my grapevines nearly brought me to tears. Stripped bare, they looked naked and pitiful. All that remained were the central vines and the branches closest to them. If all I wanted were leaves, this wouldn't have been necessary, but pruning is the price of fruitfulness.

To get to the heart of our worship, we may need to cut away the leaves—things that are attractive but not necessarily productive. We may have to do away with songs we love but that are not serving our church bodies. We may have to tone down certain sounds or effects. We may have to let certain musicians go or disappoint some attendees. This will be painful, but if we stay focused on the true vine, we will learn what to add back in and what to keep out for the sake of long-term fruitfulness.

Water Deeply

Mature grapevines need just enough water to reach their deep roots. When they have been thoroughly watered, they may "bleed" from recently pruned branches. This excess water heals their cuts and is drinkable.

We are less hardy; we need daily watering if we want to pour ourselves out in worship. While singing together is an essential spiritual discipline, it cannot be our only one. We need to prioritize other ways of drinking deeply of the living water (John 7:37–39). To bear fruit that spills over into our worship, we need to be renewed and refilled through regular prayer, Bible study, and fellowship.

Give It Time

I grew antsy this spring when my grapevines showed little growth. Had last year's pruning killed them? Was the winter too harsh? I waited for weeks but only saw a bud here and there. Then, seemingly overnight, they exploded with greenery.

Psalm 1 describes a person who trusts in the Lord as "a tree planted by streams of water that yields its fruit in its season" (Ps. 1:3). *In its season.* Let's not panic when we do not experience love, joy, peace, patience, kindness, goodness, faithfulness, gentleness, and self-control all at once in every way. Like diligent gardeners, we must keep planting, watering, and pruning. Our job is to keep "sowing to the Spirit" while trusting that God will give growth in due time, so long as we do not give up (Gal. 6:8–9).

Benediction

We pray for our pastors before their sermons, but how often do we pray before singing? As we conclude, let's pray over our worship: "God Our Gardener, as we gather to lift high Christ the true vine, fill us with the Holy Spirit, that we may sing your songs and bear much fruit. Amen."

Reflection/Discussion

1. Have you experienced a time when one fruit helped produce another?

2. How might "fruitful worship" look different in your church than in other churches?

3. How would you describe your current season of worship or ministry? What other disciplines are you prioritizing?

4. Which fruit of the Spirit do you find the most challenging? The most encouraging?

5. How has considering musical worship according to the fruit of the Spirit changed or refined your approach to worship leadership or participation?

Postlude

WORSHIP SONGS have increasingly short lifespans.[1] Worship leaders seem to quit or change jobs earlier and earlier.[2] Musical methods come and go. Leadership strategies rise and fall. But you know what will never pass away? The love described by 1 Corinthians 13, which is the fruit listed in Galatians 5:22–23. When we cultivate this fruit in our musical worship, we invest in the eternal. We join in a chorus that never ends.

Jesus tells his disciples, "I chose you and appointed you that you should go and bear fruit and that your fruit should abide" (John 15:16). *Abide* means remain—*stay*. Only the followers and fruit connected to the true vine will remain forever.

The fruit of the Spirit will not fade with the latest musical trend or retire when we do. It will not sink into oblivion or become outdated. So let's sing, play, practice, lead, volunteer, and participate according to our abiding worship: love, joy, peace, patience, kindness, goodness, faithfulness, gentleness, and self-control.

1 Daniel Silliman, "We've No Less Days to Sing God's Praise, but New Worship Songs Only Last a Few Years," *Christianity Today*, November 22, 2021, https://christianitytoday.com/.

2 Alex Enfiedjian, "Worship Leader: Are You Thinking of Quitting? When to Stay, When to Quit," *Worship Ministry Training* (blog), October 8, 2023, https://www.worshipministrytraining.com/.

Acknowledgments

I THANK MY HUSBAND, Billy, for loving me enough to ask tough questions about worship, and for bearing with me through the long process of pitching and writing this book.

This book would not exist without the influence of the leaders and teachers whose discipline, enthusiasm, and humility continue to inspire me: Mrs. Webb, the Hawkinsons, Flo, Dr. Chiang, Lynnette, Dr. Hung, Dr. Stewart, the Owens, Dr. Lee, Richard, Jane, Christie—the list (and my gratitude) goes on and on.

I am especially grateful to Samuel, my developmental editor, whose advocacy brought this book into being, and Tara, whose eye for detail beautifully fine-tuned my work. I'd also like to thank my unofficial editors, the friends and family who took the time to read my manuscript and offer feedback, especially Brian, Tyler, Laura, and my former-English-teacher mother.

Finally, I thank my dear churches for their faithful prayers and wholehearted singing.

Selected Hymns

THE FOLLOWING HYMN TEXTS are public domain and can be accessed on Hymnary.org. I encourage readers to explore Hymnary, a wonderful free resource that features various versions of hymn texts, different musical settings, and background information on composers and writers.

Arends, Wilhelm Erasmus. "Rise! To Arms! With Prayer Employ You." Translated by John M. Sloan. 1714.

Byrne, Mary E., trans. "Be Thou My Vision." 1905. Versified by Eleanor H. Hull. 1912.

Chrisholm, Thomas O. "Great Is Thy Faithfulness." 1923.

Francis, S. Trevor. "O the Deep, Deep Love of Jesus!" 1890.

Havergal, Frances. "Take My Life, and Let It Be." 1874.

"How Can I Keep from Singing?" Author and date unknown.

Matheson, George. "O Love That Wilt Not Let Me Go." 1882.

Scriven, Joseph Medlicott. "What a Friend We Have in Jesus." 1855.

Monsell, John S. B. "Fight the Good Fight." 1863.

Newton, John. "Amazing Grace! (How Sweet the Sound)." 1779.

Robinson, Robert. "Come, Thou Fount of Every Blessing." 1758.

Schlegel, Kathrina von. "Be Still, My Soul." Translated by Jane Borthwick. 1752.

Watts, Isaac. "My Shepherd Will Supply My Need." 1786.

Wilkinson, Kate B. "May the Mind of Christ, My Savior." 1925.

Bibliography

Begbie, Jeremy S. *Resounding Truth: Christian Wisdom in the World of Music*. Engaging Culture. Baker Academic, 2007.

Bennett, Arthur. "The Valley of Vision." In *The Valley of Vision: A Collection of Puritan Prayers & Devotions*. Banner of Truth, 1975.

Bonhoeffer, Dietrich. *The Cost of Discipleship*. Translated by R. H. Fuller. Macmillan, 1948. Reprint, Simon & Schuster, 1995.

Bonhoeffer, Dietrich. *Life Together: The Classic Exploration of Christian Community*. Translated by John W. Doberstein. HarperOne, 1954.

Brockman, Rob. "The Art of Lament." The Gospel Coalition Canada, March 31, 2021. https://ca.thegospelcoalition.org/.

Challies, Tim. "The Mark of the Most Successful Worship Leaders," August 9, 2017. *Challies.com* (blog). https://www.challies.com/.

Crabtree, Sam. *Practicing Affirmation: God-Centered Praise of Those Who Are Not God*. Crossway, 2011.

Danker, Frederick William, ed. *A Greek-English Lexicon of the New Testament and Other Early Christian Literature*. Third Edition. University of Chicago Press, 2000.

Dennis, Lane T., and Wayne Grudem, eds. *ESV Study Bible: English Standard Version*. Crossway, 2016.

Edwards, Jonathan. *The Works of Jonathan Edwards*. Vol. 14, *Sermons and Discourses: 1723–1729*. Edited by Kenneth P. Minkema. Yale University Press, 1997.

Enfiedjian, Alex. "Worship Leader: Are You Thinking of Quitting? When to Stay, When to Quit." *Worship Ministry Training* (blog), October 8, 2023. https://www.worshipministrytraining.com.

Ferguson, Sinclair. "The Heavenly Music of Self-Control." Ligonier Ministries, February 23, 2024. https://www.ligonier.org/.

Ferguson, Sinclair B. *Maturity: Growing Up and Going On in the Christian Life*. Banner of Truth, 2019.

Franzmann, Martin H. "Hymn #578: Thy Strong Word." In *Lutheran Service Book*. Concordia, 2006.

Guthrie, Steven R. *Creator Spirit: The Holy Spirit and the Art of Becoming Human*. Baker Academic, 2011.

Guthrie, Steven R. "The Wisdom of Song." In *Resonant Witness: Conversations Between Music and Theology*, edited by Jeremy S. Begbie and Steven R. Guthrie. Eerdmans, 2011.

Harris, W. Hall, ed. *The NET Bible, Second Edition Notes*. 2nd ed. Thomas Nelson, 2019.

Hicks, Zac. "What Worship Curved in on Itself Looks Like." *Zac Hicks* (blog), November 19, 2013. https://zachicks.com/.

Jamieson, Robert, A.R. Fausset, and David Brown. *Commentary Critical and Explanatory on the Whole Bible*. Christian Classics Ethereal Library, 1871.

Julian, John. *A Dictionary of Hymnology*. Vol. 2. Dover, 1907.

Luther, Martin. *Letters II*. Edited by Gottfried G. Krodel. Vol. 49 of *Luther's Works*, American Edition. Edited by Jaroslav Pelikan and Helmut T. Lehmann. Fortress Press, 1972.

Luther, Martin. "Preface to Georg Rhau's Symphoniae Iucundae." In *Liturgy and Hymns.* Edited by Ulrich S. Leupold and Helmut T. Lehmann. Translated by Paul Zeller Strodach. Vol. 53 of *Luther's Works*, American Edition. Edited by Jaroslav Pelikan and Helmut T. Lehmann. Fortress Press, 1965.

MacMillan, James. *A Scot's Song: A Life of Music.* Birlinn Limited, 2019.

Menikoff, Aaron. "The Flesh Is Weak: Pastoral Reflections on Self-Control." 9Marks, November 16, 2017. https://www.9marks.org/.

Miate, Liana. "Horae." *World History Encyclopedia.* March 29, 2023. https://www.worldhistory.org/.

"Mission, Beliefs, and Values," KLove. Accessed October 2, 2024. https://www.klove.com.

Molinari, Ryanne. "The Season of Broken Things." *Ryanne Molinari* (blog), March 13, 2025. https://ryannemolinari.com/.

Molinari, Ryanne. "Three Reasons You Don't Feel Joyful During Musical Worship." *Ryanne Molinari* (blog), July 26, 2023. https://ryannemolinari.com/.

Molinari, Ryanne. "Three Ways Musical Roots Teach Us About Love." *Ryanne Molinari* (blog), July 14, 2023. https://ryannemolinari.com/.

Moore, Megan Bishop. "Fruit." In *Eerdman's Dictionary of the Bible*, edited by David Noel Freedman. Eerdmans, 2000.

Mounce, Bill. "Μέγας." Bill Mounce website. Accessed September 2, 2024. https://www.billmounce.com/.

Mounce, Bill. "Τιμή." Bill Mounce website. Accessed February 21, 2025. https://www.billmounce.com/.

Newton, John. *Letters of John Newton: With Biographical Sketches and Notes by Josiah Bull.* Banner of Truth, 2007.

Ortlund, Dane. *Gentle and Lowly: The Heart of Christ for Sinners and Sufferers*. Crossway, 2020.

Polman, Bert. "Joseph Medlicott Scriven." Hymnary.org. Accessed March 12, 2024. https://hymnary.org/.

Ryken, Leland. *40 Favorite Hymns on the Christian Life: A Closer Look at Their Spiritual and Poetic Meaning*. P&R, 2019.

Ryken, Philip Graham. *Art for God's Sake: A Call to Recover the Arts*. P&R, 2006.

Schaeffer, Francis A. *The Lord's Work in the Lord's Way*. In *"The Lord's Work in the Lord's Way" and "No Little People."* Crossway Short Classics. Crossway, 2022.

Shakespeare, William. "Twelfth Night; Or, What You Will." In *The Complete Works of William Shakespeare*, The Edition of The Shakespeare Head Press Oxford. Barnes & Noble, 1994.

Silliman, Daniel. "We've No Less Days to Sing God's Praise, But New Worship Songs Only Last a Few Years." *Christianity Today*, November 22, 2021. http://christianitytoday.com.

Sreenivas, Shishira, and Shawna Seed. "The Dunning-Kruger Effect: Causes, Examples, and Impact." WebMD, February 7, 2024. https://www.webmd.com/.

Tarrants, Thomas A. "Finding Power to Live a New Life: Discipleship and the Holy Spirit." *C. S. Lewis Institute* (blog), March 4, 2012. https://www.cslewisinstitute.org/.

Taylor, Justin. "Do the Next Thing." The Gospel Coalition, October 25, 2017. https://www.thegospelcoalition.org/.

Thayer, Joseph H. *Thayer's Greek-English Lexicon of the New Testament*. New York, 1889. Reprint, Hendrickson, 2023.

Trench, R. C. *Trench's Synonyms of the New Testament*. Edited by Robert G. Hoerber, John J. Hughes, and Claire M. Hughes. Baker, 1989.

Vickhoff, Björn, Helge Malmgren, Rickard Åström, Gunnar Nyberg, Mathias Engvall, Johan Snygg, Michael Nilsson, and Rebecka Jörnsten. "Music Structure Determines Heart Rate Variability of Singers." *Frontiers in Psychology* 4 (2013). https://doi.org/10.3389/fpsyg.2013.00334.

Vincent, Marvin R. *Word Studies in the New Testament.* Vols. 1, 3, and 4. Charles Scribner's Sons, 1887.

Watson, Christopher. "Worship in the Average Church in America." *Worship Leader* (blog), June 27, 2023. https://worshipleader.com/.

Weidmann, Josh. "The Blind Preacher Who Saw Quite Well: A Short Bio of George Matheson." *Josh Weidmann* (blog). Accessed October 2, 2024. https://joshweidmann.com/.

Wenham, G. J., J. A. Motyer, D. A. Carson , and R. T. France, eds. *Matthew.* New Bible Commentary: 21st Century Edition. InterVarsity Press, 1994. Accordance.

Spirit-Filled Singing Playlist

A playlist to accompany this book can be accessed by scanning the QR code below, searching "Spirit-Filled Listening (Crossway)" on Spotify, or using the following URL: https://open.spotify.com/playlist/3eUAPo58pzHxWILp3s5Uhw?si=d7b98c4bc8b648e9

General Index

Scripture Index